DREAMS COME TRUE

THE 75 YEAR HISTORY OF

HILCO ELECTRIC COOPERATIVE, INC.

1937 - 2012

DREAMS COME TRUE

THE 75 YEAR HISTORY OF
HILCO ELECTRIC COOPERATIVE, INC.
1937 - 2012

---

by

Brian K. Moreland

Itasca, TX

Acknowledgements

There are a number of people I wish to thank for helping with this book. First, thanks to the HILCO employees I interviewed for sharing your time and personal stories: Dub Stout, William Watson, Bob Wilson, Wesley Brackin and his wife Rose Marie, David Brackin, Kenneth Upchurch, Ronnie Upchurch, Crystal Upchurch, Milton Cranfill, Larry Farquhar, Tommy Cox, Gary Lewis, Rhonda Trejo, Gena Brooks, Travis Sanders, Lea Sanders, and Debbie Cole. Special thanks to Billy Gene Farrow for sharing so many wonderful stories about his father, Earl Farrow, and filling in a lot of the Co-op's early history. Thank you to Margaret Rhea for helping me gather photos from the archives and to Jill Huggins for scanning photos. Many thanks to Debbie Cole and Lea Sanders for all your help producing this book every step of the way. And thank you to HILCO's board of directors — President Bill Allen, Vice President George Thiess, Secretary / Treasurer Margaret Hill, Janet Smith, Ron Roberts, Stephen Pape, Joseph Tedesco—for choosing me to research and write your 75-year history book.

Contents

Foreword   *xi*

Preface   *xiii*

Chapter One: The Dream Begins   1

Chapter Two: Earl D.H. Farrow   5

Chapter Three: The 1930s   11

Chapter Four: The 1940s   37

Chapter Five: The 1950s   59

Chapter Six: The 1960s   69

Chapter Seven: The 1970s   103

Chapter Eight: The 1980s   119

Chapter Nine: The 1990s   145

Chapter Ten: The 2000s   169

Chapter Eleven: 2012 and Beyond   219

Appendix: The People of HILCO   223

Foreword

The HILCO Board of Directors is proud of the history of HILCO Electric Cooperative, and in order to preserve the history for all our past and future Members, we have recorded the 75-year history of the Cooperative. Our electric co-op, originally named Hill County Electric Cooperative, was incorporated in 1937 by the founding general manager, Earl D. H. Farrow, and the first board of directors to deliver power to rural farmers. This book captures what people in rural America were going through back in the early 1900s, how the need for cooperatives came about, and how HILCO began and evolved into the company we are today. The year 2012 marks our 75th year serving our Members.

HILCO's Board of Directors, from top left: Ron Roberts, Joseph Tedesco, Stephen Pape, Vice President George Thiess, Secretary/Treasurer Margaret Hill, President Bill Allen, and Janet Smith

Preface

About ten years ago I was visiting my parents at their new home in Whitney, Texas. They live in a beautiful golf resort community called White Bluff that resides on the cliffs that overlook Lake Whitney. I noticed my mother was reading a magazine called *Texas Co-op Power*. On the cover was a photo of some power lines with ranch land in the background. Curious, I asked Mom what the magazine was about. She said it was full of articles discussing the electric cooperative industry and that the magazine kept co-op members (which included my mom and dad) up to date on the advances in the electric power industry. I laughed and jokingly said, "How in the world could reading about electric power be interesting?" Mom just smiled and said she enjoyed the articles and helpful tips on how to conserve energy.

As fate would have it ten years later, HILCO Electric Cooperative, a power company that publishes articles in that very magazine my mother reads, invited me to write a book documenting the 75-year history of their electric co-op. Now, while I am known for writing historical novels, I love history in general and was intrigued by the project, so I took on the challenge of researching and writing the book. Once again I was faced with the question: What's interesting about an electric power company? How can I tell a story that is fascinating and will grip readers like a great novel?

I went in search of answers as I drove from the big city of Dallas down to Itasca, a small town tucked away in the farm country of Central Texas. Now, I'll be the first to admit that before writing this book, I knew little about the power industry. I didn't even know what an electric cooperative was. I paid my electric bill every month and that was about the most thought I gave it. Power lines had been for the most part invisible to me. The only time I noticed them was when a hawk would land on one of the T-shaped poles. Even as I was driving to Itasca that first time, the poles and wires that stretch on either side of the interstate highway remained in my peripheral vision. I never thought much about the electric power that runs along those lines, where it originated from or where it ended, or even who built those power lines that run across America. My whole life electricity had always been available and something I took for granted.

When I arrived into Central Texas on a hot day in May, the heat was shimmering across the cattle fields. I turned west off of I-35, drove past a Dairy Queen and into the remote town of Itasca. My first impression was I had driven back in time to the days when life was simple. Itasca is quaint, peaceful, and moves at a pace much slower than the hustle and bustle of Dallas. I didn't even see another car as I drove down the main street. I found HILCO's headquarters at the center of town. The main office has a cozy and inviting front lobby with cubicles of friendly office staff and a broad wood staircase that leads to the second floor offices. All the employees I met welcomed me with the kind of hospitality you only find in small towns.

I was taken to the board room where I met with General Manager Debbie Cole and Assistant Manager Lea Sanders.

They spoke proudly of their Co-op and showed me countless photos that made up the history of HILCO, which I learned was originally Hill County Electric Cooperative. I saw black and white photos and yellow newspaper articles about the company's founder and original manager, Earl. D. H. Farrow. I learned that the company started back in the Thirties when the rural farms south of Dallas didn't have electricity. Come to find out this electric power that I had always taken for granted wasn't always available. For the farmers and ranchers and even a few rural towns, light bulbs and power sockets were just luxuries they dreamed of one day having. But back before the 1930s, electric power companies only delivered power to the cities and towns.

During my research, I sifted through decades of photos of the people who have worked at the Co-op over the course of 75 years: linemen, office staff, dispatchers, meter readers, superintendents, general managers, board members, and the members themselves. I discovered that what sets HILCO Electric Cooperative apart from other electric utility companies is HILCO is a non-profit company that is made up of customers who are also members. The money they pay toward their utility bills covers the costs of running the electric cooperative. The profits get redistributed back to the members and a portion gets donated to charities and student scholarships. More than financial rewards, there is a great sense of community as HILCO hosts member picnics twice a year. The members even vote for the board of directors who oversees the Co-op to make sure it's always working in the best interest of its members. There is also a family atmosphere among the Co-op's employees that you don't find in today's corporate world.

Over the course of the summer I interviewed over twenty employees who were a real cast of characters. Some who had worked in the Forties, Fifties, and Sixties had already retired. Many had been working at HILCO for well over twenty years, some over thirty. Their stories had me laughing and often times amazed at what I was hearing. Soon I began to see that there is so much more to this book than writing about electric power.

I also had the pleasure of driving down to San Antonio and interviewing Earl Farrow's son, Gene Farrow. From him I gained a vast understanding of what Earl Farrow had to endure in his early days of starting the company. And the more I learned about the man behind it all, the more I discovered a true hero who played a major role in building those power lines I now see stretching on either side of the highway.

Once I gathered all my research, I had my answer of what it is that makes the history of an electric power cooperative fascinating. This is a collection of stories about people going after dreams, enduring human struggle, celebrating triumphs, and living out wild adventures in Central Texas. I invite you to journey back over 75 years and discover how one man's dream brought power to so many people.

Brian K. Moreland

"It is the obvious duty of the Government to call the attention of farmers to the growing monopolization of water power. The farmers above all should have that power, on reasonable terms, for cheap transportation, for lighting their homes, and for innumerable uses in the daily tasks on the farm."

—President Theodore Roosevelt
Message to Congress
The Country Life Commission Report
February 9, 1909

CHAPTER ONE

The Dream Begins

The dream to bring power to the rural people didn't begin with a light bulb of inspiration. Nor did it begin with utility companies building power lines to every house in the nation. The dream started with President Teddy Roosevelt's recognition that Rural America was suffering. In the early 1900s, millions of farmers, ranchers, and inhabitants of remote towns were cut off from the utility companies that delivered power to America's cities. Improving the working and living conditions of the rural people became a great social concern, as well as a need to conserve the nation's agriculture industry.

To create a long-term solution, President Roosevelt appointed the Commission on Country Life in 1908. The board's mission was to gather facts on how the quality of rural living was falling behind while life in the cities was progressing into the twentieth century. The country's greatest problem, the commission concluded, was that Rural America lacked electric power to light their farms and sustain a decent living.

The dream to bring power to the rural people started as a spark of hope for one young Texas farmer, as sixteen-year-old Earl Farrow witnessed a wondrous event. On a hot and dusty summer day in 1911, while working in the cotton fields of his father's mid-Texas farm, Earl noticed a group of workers constructing power lines a quarter mile down the road. The local utility company, Texas Power and Light, was stringing wire to the homes in Itasca, a small town in Hill County.

Upon seeing the progress that was happening, Earl looked back at his parents' farm house. The Farrow's were sharecropper farmers living on a stretch of land that grew cotton, a variety of vegetables, and orchards of fruit trees. They had never enjoyed the glory of power that benefited people living in the cities and towns. Rural life was still as challenging as how the pioneers had lived in the 1800s. The only light to ever shine in the Farrow house was from candles and kerosene lamps. At night, most of the house was in darkness. Like their rural neighbors, the Farrows had to do everything by hand, from washing laundry to pumping water from a well. Without power, they couldn't store their food in a refrigerator. To keep meat and milk fresh, they had to buy ice for their icebox. Fruits and vegetables had to be preserved in jars. This work was especially hard on the women, who handled the household chores. While the men worked the fields and brought in the crops, the women had to jar the fruits and vegetables before they spoiled.

Without power, farmers couldn't heat their homes. They had to cut wood daily and burn it in their fireplaces and wood-burning stoves. They couldn't pump water into their houses, so bathing was done in metal tubs, and toilets were typically outhouses. Without electricity, the rural people couldn't use any of the appliances that were being advertised in the newspapers and magazines. Blenders, sewing machines, washing machines, radios, and electric stoves were luxury items for the city people. For the farmers, it seemed, life would always be burdened with hard work and struggle.

The sight of power lines being built around the edge of Itasca must have been like witnessing a miracle to young Earl Farrow. He drove to where the linemen were working and asked if they would build a line to his father's farm. But his request was denied, because Texas Power and Light would not provide service that far outside of town. It would cost too much money to build miles of poles and wire just to power a few rural farmhouses.

Frustrated, Earl returned home with a burning in his chest to figure out some way to get power distributed to his parents' farm. His mother and father had endured hard work their whole lives and deserved to enjoy the conveniences of a home powered by electricity. On that fateful day, as young Earl Farrow dreamed of what was possible for the rural people, he had no idea he was about to begin a life journey that would impact so many lives.

CHAPTER TWO

Earl D. H. Farrow

As Earl Farrow graduated from high school and developed into a young man, his lofty dreams were put on hold as his nation had bigger issues to tackle. In 1917, World War I was heating up over in Europe. Great Britain, France, and Russia were suffering numerous casualties in a trench war against formidable German-Hungarian forces. The United States had done their best to stay out of the war, practicing their policy of nonintervention, but then on April 6, 1917, President Wilson and Congress declared war on Germany.

At age twenty-two, Earl Farrow decided to serve his country and joined the Navy. After attending boot camp in San Diego, he traveled by train to New York, where ships were waiting to carry the sailors over to Europe. During the cross-country journey, his train stopped for fuel and water in Salisbury, North Carolina. Normally the military personnel were allowed to disembark, but on this particular day the train was quarantined, and everyone had to stay on board. Earl was standing guard at one of the doors, when a young Red Cross volunteer by the name of Pauline Loflin came up and talked to him. The lady volunteers were nicknamed "Cookie Girls," because their jobs were to give out cookies to the soldiers. Since Earl was the only sailor outside the train, Pauline talked to him for an hour. That was enough time to fire off sparks in Earl's heart. As the train was starting to leave, he got Pauline's address and told her, "After the war's over, I'm coming back to make you my wife."

Earl spent the next two years serving in the Great War, working and living on his Navy ship overseas, but he never forgot about that "Cookie Girl" back in North Carolina. During his duty he wrote letters to Pauline and she responded back.

Over in Europe, the U.S. forces aided the allies in the trench wars, pummeling the German armies and driving them back. World War I finally ended in late 1918 with a German cease fire. The U.S. soldiers came home victorious. In 1919, at age twenty-four, Earl Farrow completed his tour with the Navy and returned home to Itasca, Texas. He continued to write Pauline. After almost three years and countless love letters, Earl finally traveled back to North Carolina to fulfill his promise to make Pauline his bride. They married on Christmas Eve in 1919, and on Christmas morning they left for Texas to start their life together.

In the post-war era, the 1920s was a period of economic strength in America. Major league baseball became a favorite pastime, and Babe Ruth, the home-run king of the New York Yankees, was already a legendary baseball player. The prohibition of alcohol ignited an explosion of Mafia crimes led by famous mobsters like Al Capone and "Bugs" Moran. Silent movies created the first movie stars in Charlie Chaplin, Greta Garbo, and Douglas Fairbanks. Liberated young women flaunted their wild spirits as "flappers," wearing short skirts, bobbed hair, smoking cigarettes and dancing the Charleston at nightclubs, as the Jazz Age was in full swing.

Meanwhile, far from the glitz and glamour of big cities,

Earl and Pauline Farrow lived a quiet existence at his parents' sharecropping farm. Earl made a meager living farming for his father and doing odd jobs around town. It was rough living. Despite the fact that all the houses in nearby Itasca had power, the Farrow farm was still out of reach of the power lines, even though they could see Texas Power and Light's substation near the far corner of their land. The farmers were at the mercy of the investor-owned utility companies, so the Farrows and their neighbors continued to farm without power.

In 1921, Earl did a temporary job paving the streets of Itasca. While he was out working one day, a businessman, by the name of Grover Brown, offered him a job to work as a salesman in his furniture store. Earl happily accepted the opportunity to work his first full-time job. With the stability of earning a steady paycheck, he and Pauline moved off the farm and into a small apartment in Itasca. It was his first home powered by electricity. The rooms were lit by light bulbs and there were power sockets for appliances. Earl had finally achieved modern living.

Back then, Itasca was a small town with a population of around 1800. The town was named after Lake Itasca, which is the headwaters of the Mississippi River. Earl found this fact interesting, so he drove Pauline up to Minnesota to see Lake Itasca. They were planning to vacation there a week. They stayed one night and the next day Earl looked at the lake and said, "Well, I've seen it. Let's go." Just like that they packed up and headed back home. Earl was never one to stay idle too long.

In 1926, he decided the town needed an undertaker. So he drove up to Dallas and spent three months getting certified to be an embalmer and mortician. He returned to Itasca and continued to sell furniture for Mr. Brown, and when someone in town passed away, Earl worked as the undertaker. He did the embalming upstairs in the back section of the Brown-Reese building. People would shop for furniture downstairs and, if they happened to need a casket, Earl had several stored upstairs in the funeral parlor.

For the next couple of years he focused on his career and family. He and Pauline had two boys, John Earl and Billy Gene. Earl's youngest son, Gene, remembers what his father was like, "He was a good father. He was firm. He was a good task master . . . a friend for life. He was loyal to his people."

Earl Farrow became very active in the community. He served as deacon in the First Presbyterian Church, the church treasurer, and superintendent of the Sunday school. Earl seemed to gravitate toward roles of leadership. In 1928, at the age of thirty-three, he was elected as mayor of Itasca. The job of running the town paid a paltry fifty dollars a year. To make a decent living, he continued to sell furniture for Mr. Brown and work as a mortician.

The plaque that always sat on Mr. Farrow's desk

As Earl served his term as mayor, he must have recognized that the lack of infrastructure to deliver power to the farmers' homes was causing an extreme rift between the quality of urban and rural living. While the flappers danced in the city nightclubs and Babe Ruth hit home runs, there seemed to be no end to America's economic boom. But for the rural people, the 1920s proved to be a decade of struggle. Droughts and dust storms destroyed their crops. Poverty and despair were twin evils that burdened the farming communities, and there was little government reform to aid their losses. The rise of the Industrial Revolution provided more opportunities to work in factories, mills, and areas of heavy commerce. The agricultural industry became even more crippled as young farm workers fled to the cities in search of better jobs and a higher standard of living. Many rural families, fed up with battling the dust storms and droughts, abandoned their farms completely.

While Mayor Farrow was working steady enough to endure these hard times, he saw his rural neighbors were struggling as the industry of agriculture went into further decline. His unyielding duty to the local people, the farmers, his country, and a deep faith in God fueled his passion to help bring power to those beyond the borders of his town.

"I pledge you—I pledge myself to a New Deal for the American People."

— President Franklin Delano Roosevelt

July 1932

CHAPTER THREE

The 1930s:
The Dawn of Rural Electrification

The drought that was blighting the rural communities during the 1920s eventually caught up with the city dwellers, and the decade of economic prosperity came to an end. With the crash of the stock market on October 29, 1929, also known as "Black Tuesday," America entered the 1930s in turmoil and poverty on a national scale that would become known as The Great Depression. The financial lending system spiraled downward, as banks closed one after another. The remaining bankers panicked and hoarded billions of dollars in currency and gold. As a result, many businesses shut down and houses and farms were foreclosed. Millions of people found themselves without jobs as unemployment rose to twenty-five percent. Across the nation, men and women became homeless and struggled to feed their families. Retired Hill County Electric employee, Dub Stout, remembers those days, "People didn't have jobs anywhere, especially in this part of the country, because there weren't any factories down here."

The desperate masses migrated across the country like gypsies in search of work, competing for odd jobs picking fruit in orchards or harvesting crops in the fields. But work remained scarce, because farming and rural areas suffered as crop prices plummeted and numerous farms shut down. The farming industry wasn't the only one in deep decline. Lumber-mill towns like Manning, Texas and Pine Valley, Oklahoma were abandoned and became ghost towns. The economic depression in America hit rock bottom by late 1933 and was so severe that it spread worldwide, affecting every country around the globe.

A farm family during The Great Depression

In the United States, newly-elected President Franklin Delano Roosevelt faced this travesty head-on in 1933. After giving his famous inaugural speech, "The only thing we have to fear is fear itself," he introduced his economic recovery solution called "The New Deal." His aggressive approach to reform focused on implementing government relief programs within the first hundred days of Roosevelt's presidency. Congress united with the president's vision and passed many of the New Deal programs, concentrating on the three R's: relief of unemployment, recovery of the economic system, and reform of the financial institutions.

Like former president Teddy Roosevelt, FDR had a keen interest in improving Rural America. In his address at French Lick, Indiana in 1931, he said, "The possibility of diversifying our industrial life by sending a fair proportion of it into the rural districts is one of the definite possibilities of the future. Cheap electric power, good roads, and automobiles make such a rural development possible."

The New Deal opened up the floodgates for other conservationists to focus on the livelihood of the rural communities. One advocate for change, Morris L. Cooke, went to Washington and lobbied to reform the agricultural industry through rural electrification. If the farmers continued to quit farming due to poor working conditions, there would be no one left to supply food to the nation. In his request that the government devise a plan for national electrification, Cooke wrote a document called, "This Report Can Be Read in 12 Minutes." With a powerful argument, he stated his case:

WHY RURAL ELECTRIFICATION IMPORTANT

Agriculture is a major problem. It must evolve toward the status of a dignified and self-sustaining sector of our social life. So agriculture demands all the pertinent production and comfort facilities now available to the industry.

WHAT IS THE TASK?

Of the six million farms in the United States, over 800,000 are "electrified." But only about 650,000 have "high-line" service . . . Over 5,000,000 farms are entirely without electric service.

ADVANTAGES OF RURAL ELECTRIFICATION

Both for the farmer and his wife the introduction of electricity goes a long way toward the elimination of drudgery. The electric refrigerator will effect a considerable change in diet—more fresh vegetables and less salt and cured meats. The inside bathroom, made possible by automatic electric pumping, brings to the farm one of the major comforts of urban life.

"Most of the community didn't have lights," recalls Dub Stout. "Kerosene lamps was the main thing. Some of them had these Delco units. Most of them had storm cellars, and they didn't have heat, so they had to sleep in storm cellars at night. If they had a kerosene stove they were uptown, modern . . . Most of them cooked with wood and heated with wood. We used to have to cut wood for the fireplace, and if you've ever had to cut wood for a fireplace, it was a full-time job. That was the life of the farmer then."

Morris Cooke's "Twelve-Minute" document discussed in length the daily issues of the farmer trying to work without electricity and how this affected the nation as a whole. His plan was for the government to distribute cheap electricity to the rural people. "This proposal does not involve competition with private interests," Cooke's proposal emphasized. "This plan calls for entering territory not now occupied and not likely to be occupied to any considerable intent by the private interests." In essence, Cooke wanted the government to build power lines across the countless miles of rural country to the farms that the investor-owned utility companies refused to reach. The document offered concrete solutions on how to deliver power to the rural people. Cooke's answer: form a new rural electrification agency.

Morris Cooke's lobbying convinced President Roosevelt rural electrification fit right in with his New Deal programs, and on May 11, 1935, FDR signed an executive order to form the Rural Electrification Administration as a relief agency. Cooke headed up the REA as the administrator. His task: build a nation-wide infrastructure to electrify over five million farms. This was to be done through hiring workers to build power lines off of existing substations controlled by the private interest utility companies. But just months into the program, Cooke dealt with bureaucratic resistance to giving his program the proper funding to hire a work force and buy all the equipment. As a result, he decided the REA would operate more efficiently as a lending agency. FDR agreed. The newly reformed REA was set up to loan money to existing businesses who would build the power lines. Cooke requested the help from the privately owned utility companies in branching off from their substations. The REA continued to struggle to make headway, however, as the leaders of the power companies only wanted to use the government funding to help connect a small sector of farmers close to their substations, neglecting the millions of rural people that had farms in the more remote regions. The power companies even tried to thwart Cooke's efforts, by lobbying that the government had no right to compete in the utility business.

A gathering of farmers

The farmers and ranchers, who were desperate to electrify their rural communities, formed a grass roots movement that got behind the REA's mission to provide rural electrification. The farmers formed cooperatives, offering to build the power lines themselves. Morris Cooke received loan applications by the hundreds and realized lending money to farming cooperatives might be the best solution for electrifying Rural America. The REA administrator just had to convince Washington that this was the best route.

Three other key advocates who aided Cooke's mission were Senator George W. Norris of Nebraska, Representative Sam Rayburn of Texas, and Representative John E. Rankin of Mississippi. In early 1936, they proposed a bill to Congress to make the REA a permanent agency authorized to give out loans to the cooperatives. For several months the House and Senate debated over the bill. The relentless efforts of Senator Norris and Representatives Rayburn and Rankin got the bill passed through the House and Senate by May 15, 1936. Six days later President Roosevelt signed the Rural Electrification Act.

Representative John Rankin, President Franklin Delano Roosevelt, and Senator George W. Norris

The REA was now set up to provide loans to the cooperatives to install power lines and distribute electricity to the rural people. Operating the cooperatives as non-profit businesses, the farmers and ranchers elected boards who represented the members, voted on the rates per kilowatt, and hired the co-op managers. The income earned from the sales of the electricity would pay off the government loans and any "profits" would go back to its members. Morris Cooke's vision had created a brilliant win-win for the government and the rural people.

Hundreds of loan applications were fulfilled, and the construction of new power lines got underway, but there were still numerous counties that didn't have organized co-ops. So the REA set out on a new mission to find individual leaders across the country who were willing to head up rural electric cooperatives.

One of the first REA Co-ops

While all this change was happening at a national level, down south in Hill County of Central Texas, Earl Farrow was busy raising his two sons, being a deacon at his church, selling furniture, and working as a mortician. He served eight years as Mayor of Itasca, doing his part to keep the town from blowing away with the dust storms like so many small towns during the Depression. Little did Mr. Farrow know, his career was about to change radically in the summer of 1936, when a man from the REA showed up at his door.

An Extraordinary Opportunity

Ad campaign for the REA

The REA representative from Washington approached Earl Farrow because he was the mayor of Itasca. The man asked if Earl would be interested in getting the local farmers to sign a petition for electric service. Remembering the drudgery of farming without power, Earl accepted the task and went around the area petitioning farmers. After he got a good number of them signed up, the man from the REA offered Earl a job working as organizing manager for the rural electric cooperative for the area. The co-op would be headquartered in nearby Hillsboro, Texas, the county seat, and responsible for the rural parts of Hill County, as well as cover territory in four other counties.

If Earl accepted the job, he would receive $150,000 in seed money. His challenge, however, was he would have to quit working at the furniture store and work full-time for the REA without pay for the first six months. His only source of income was that he could still do the embalming part time.

That night, Earl gathered his family together and talked about the opportunity. His wife, Pauline, said, "Whatever you want to do." Gene Farrow remembers his father's dilemma. "He didn't know how he was going to handle this six months with no income. So, I guess the next day after he talked to the guy, he told him he'd get back with him as quick as he could."

That same day, Earl discussed the matter over breakfast with his three closest friends. Frank Davis, who ran the local grocery store, told Earl, "Well, I'll run a grocery bill for you for that time until you get the money." Will Hooks, who was a banker, offered, "If you need money, we'll lend you some." And Salty Girault, who owned an auto repair shop, said, "I've got a truck down here you can use and I'll give you gas."

With his family's support and his basic needs taken care of by his friends, Earl told the REA he'd start up the rural electric cooperative and manage it, but under one condition: "The only way I'll do it is if you make me a written promise that the Co-op will keep their headquarters in Itasca." They agreed to his request, and just like that Earl Farrow set out to fulfill his dream to deliver power to his rural neighbors.

Getting Started

During the fall and winter of 1936, Mr. Farrow focused on getting the cooperative up and running. He named the non-profit utility company "Hill County Electric Cooperative." He set up an office in a small building next to a barber shop. He hired two people right away. Salty's wife, Catherine "Kitty" Girault, worked as the secretary, and Claude Johns drove around the county signing up people to join the Co-op.

Mr. Farrow at work in his first office

Since the REA required that cooperative members be represented by a board of directors, Earl chose farmers who were from different areas and appointed them to be the first board members: Claude Wakefield, the first chairman, as well as, C.W. Johns, George G. Russell, Roy McKey, and F.W. McCown. The board met regularly in the fall of 1936, voting on what rates to charge, what salary to pay the manager, and drew up the articles of incorporation.

**Mr. Farrow with first board members
C. W. Johns (far left) and Claude Wakefield (center)**

The first loan check from the REA finally arrived toward the end of the year. Gene Farrow, who was just a boy then, remembers the day his father took him down to the local café where several townspeople were drinking coffee. "Dad told the waitress, 'I want the check for all these people.' And he told the girl, 'Can you cash this check for me to buy the coffee?' And she said, 'Mr. Farrow, what are you talking about?' And he showed her the check for $150,000." That was a glorious day for Earl Farrow. After celebrating with the townspeople over coffee, he deposited the check in the bank and paid back everyone he owed.

With the money to fund construction, Mr. Farrow hired a contractor, A.G. Ainsworth, to build the first power line. The poles and wire went up along a country road to Files Valley, where a dozen farmers were eagerly awaiting power. With their membership, they were entitled to three or four light bulbs per house.

A.G. Ainsworth's company wired the houses, installing lights and sockets, and ran a line from their house to the poles that connected to a substation at the corner of town. Texas Power & Light was the main supplier of electricity in the area, so the Co-op purchased electricity from them and distributed it across the lines to the members.

First house to receive electricity

For some farmers Christmas came early on December 21, 1936, when the first section of houses received power. "I remember that afternoon," says Gene Farrow, who was just a boy walking alongside his father. "It was almost dark and they energized the first homes. And they had gone ahead and told everybody what was coming, and I remember we would go down to each one of the houses to make sure those lights were burning. And we came to this one house and it was still dark. We went into the house, and Dad said, 'Is something wrong with the electricity?' And they said, 'No, we're afraid to turn it on.' It was just a raw light hanging down with a light bulb, and they didn't know about electricity. So Dad reached up and turned on the light . . . They were sitting there with an oil lamp or two and all of the sudden this light bulb comes on and the whole room lit up. It was like a new world." Powering the first homes was a victory for Mr. Farrow's new cooperative, which at the time had only three employees.

Five months later, on May 4, 1937, the board members made Hill County Electric Cooperative, Inc. official by signing the articles of incorporation. Four days later they voted unanimous that Earl Farrow remain the manager. At the Co-op's inception, he had no knowledge about how electricity worked and didn't know much about running a utility business. According to Gene, his father "knew how to turn on lights and he could do a few things. He just knew how to manage people and run an organization and build it up." For Mr. Farrow, he had finally reached a point in his career that he could bring about a substantial improvement to the lives of the farmers in his area.

Building the Lines

Not long after the first houses were powered, Hill County Electric moved from the small office up to a portion of the Brown-Reese building where Mr. Farrow used to sell furniture. He continued to work part-time as a mortician and did embalming upstairs. After using a contractor for a while, Mr. Farrow decided Hill County Electric should have its own construction crew to build and repair the lines. He hired Red Hobbs, Chester Upchurch, and Claude Cottingame to be the Co-op's first linemen. They dug the holes, set the poles, and strung the wire across three-phase lines that stretched for miles across the county. Wherever there were farm communities who needed power, the linemen built lines out to them. It was grueling work, especially during the hot Texas summers. A good part of their job was working high up on the poles. Their climbing gear was a belt and a set of hooks clamped to their boots that they dug into the pole as they climbed. Back then there were higher risks of electrocution and falling off a pole, because the linemen didn't have the safety equipment and training that they have today.

Mr. Farrow learned a lot about electricity that first year, and he was willing to roll up his sleeves and help out the linemen. He never worked high up on the lines, but he did climb a few poles just to see what it was like. Gene Farrow says, "I remember him coming home and telling Mom he had scrapes when he slipped off the pole. He was not afraid to go out to stake lines, and he did some of that."

Throughout the summer of 1937, Hill County Electric continued to build more power lines from Itasca's substation. In August, Mr. Farrow ran an article in the Itasca paper to prepare people for the power lines that were coming their way.

Wire Your Houses Now

Manager Farrow of the Hill County Co-operative, advises that all parties along the lines now being built and those who are expecting t o connect with the power lines, should have their homes wired without delay. If house is wired and meter deposit paid, t h e construction company will bring service wire directly to the house. Furthermore,

Saturday Socials

As the surrounding farms began working with power, a new type of social gathering formed among the members. "Saturday was the big day in town," recalls Gene Farrow. "All the farmers came to Itasca . . . and (the Co-op) had this store open and they would give classes to people on how to run line or get somebody to put in plugs . . . And they sold appliances to the farmers, so they could not only see, but have an electric stove, electric refrigerator—instead of an icebox—and mixers and all kinds of appliances . . . At that time the farmers needed an education on the use of milking machines and things like that. They would give classes to the women and the farmers on how to use all these things and that helped (Hill County Electric), because they would need more electricity, and they would get a bigger bill."

Since some of the rural members were still new to having electricity in their homes, it made for some humorous calls to the Co-op for assistance. Former lineman William Watson says, "One of the oldest stories I remember, actually it happened before I got here. There was a neighbor of ours who had built a line through our part of the county. A lady got electricity and got her a new refrigerator, and a few weeks later one of the guys went by and stopped and asked how she's liking her new refrigerator, and she said, 'Oh, it's okay. It just won't quit making ice. I've got everything full of ice in the house. And I'm throwing it out in the yard.' She didn't realize that you just let that ice freeze and then sit there until you use it. She thought when that ice tray got frozen, she had to pour the ice out, fill it up with water, and start another one."

Bob Wilson of the marketing department recalls, "A friend of mine's mother grew up in a house here on one of the first lines put in and they got their icebox. The ice trays used to be metal. And she picked up the ice tray and stuck it to her tongue. They had to take her to the doctor and it took all night."

Mr. Farrow's First Big Loss

In the late 1930s, tragedy struck the Hill County Electric family when lineman Claude Cottingame was electrocuted. "What happened there was a line was out," remembers retired lineman Wesley Brackin, "and they had to kill it out . . . It was just a short tap. And for some reason (Cottingame) went on up and was going to start working before they ever cut it off. And he got a hold of it and that was it. He's the only man we ever lost." The death of Claude Cottingame probably hit Mr. Farrow the hardest as he realized that every day there were safety hazards that put the lives of his crew in danger.

Not long after, Ralph Bailey came on board full time as the local heat man, because he had experience working with electricity at another utility company. Ralph worked in the office as Mr. Farrow's right-hand man.

Ralph Bailey

As well-respected leaders, Mr. Farrow and Ralph Bailey worked as a great team, overseeing the expansion of power lines across the rural areas surrounding Itasca. Retired lineman Dub Stout remembers, "Ralph was a good man. I did things for him and he'd do things for me. It was just a good relationship. He was just as good a man as Mr. Farrow. He and his wife didn't have any children, but Ralph always used the Co-op as his family. Every employee was part of the family. And that's the way he was."

Race to Tokio

Back in 1939, Hill County Electric didn't have exclusive rights to the territory that they were given by the REA. The open farmland of Central Texas was free game for their supplier and competitor, Texas Power & Light, to build lines to the rural communities. Mr. Farrow and the man who ran TP&L were both friends as well as rival enemies. They would often compete in the same territories for new business. If there was a community that needed power, the rule was whoever built line out to that community first got them as customers, because by law utility companies couldn't cross each other's lines. Sometimes winning these races became more about pride than gaining new customers.

There was a small town at a crossroads named "Tokio" that needed power. The "town" was not much more than a general store, gas station, and post office. At the time, the linemen of Hill County Electric were building lines out of nearby West and Abbott to some of the rural houses, so Tokio was in reach. Claude Johns had scouted out the area and told Mr. Farrow, "Earl, Texas Power and Light is going to start building power out to Tokio from another direction." This news got Mr. Farrow fired up, because whichever utility company got Tokio lit up first would win their business. That night he gathered up his crew, got pole digging machines, pole setters, and bales of wire. They got to work, building a line out of Abbott.

Mr. Farrow told his nine-year-old son, Gene, and his friend, Paul Crawford, to come help stake the lines. Gene remembers, "I didn't get paid for it. It was part of being my father's son. He got me up at five so we'd be out there at first light. What we had to do was go out and on the right-of-way that we had already gotten . . . and put stakes down where the poles were to go. And Paul and I would have a hundred-foot line, and we'd take it and walk it and mark off."

As soon as the boys marked where the poles would go, the pole digger came in and drilled the holes. Next came the pole setters, who set the poles and tamped them in, and then put guides on them. Gene says, "And then the wire stringers would put in the tops. And so we'd start at five o'clock (in the morning) and by four-thirty that afternoon we had gotten power to Tokio and cut off TP&L, because as much as they were building out, that was as far as they could go. Because the rule was in their war (whoever) got (to the cut-off point) first could go on from there. So you could build a line and that would cut off TP&L from heading farther out from West." Not only did Mr. Farrow use this "cutting-off" tactic to win Tokio, but he used it to win the Whitney area, as well.

Winds of Change

In 1939, in addition to managing Hill County Electric, Mr. Far-row was also an elder of the church and superintendent of the Sunday school. The old church that was there had moved out to the cotton mill. They had built a Sunday school building and still owed money on it. The man that owned the building said, "If y'all don't pay me off pretty soon, I'm gonna bring hay out here and store my building with hay and take it back."

Gene Farrow recalls, "Dad called a meeting between Sunday school and church, and he got up and told them what was happening and that they had to pay off that note. They owed maybe $5,000, something very small. And he said, 'To get things started, I pledge $500.' And my mother said she almost fell to the floor. 'Where are we going to get $500 to pledge to pay off the church note?' (Dad) said, 'The Lord will take care of it.' And it must have been just the next week or two, that the board of directors had their annual meeting. And Dad came home and he was smiling. "The Board gave me a $50 raise. That'll take care of the pledge." And then he said, 'God has his way of doing things.'"

Mr. Farrow was a man of integrity and he believed if there was a need for money, he could raise it or had faith that God would provide. As Hill County Electric continued to build lines out to rural houses, the number of customers increased and so did the cooperative's revenues. On December 15, 1939, Mr. Farrow made the first loan payment of $1,877.16 to the REA.

As the 1930s were coming to a close, and FDR's New Deal programs got America back on its feet, Hill County Electric gained momentum as an electric cooperative. Mr. Farrow was successful at providing power to farmers and small towns throughout five Texas counties, but unfortunately he never achieved his original dream to power to his parents' farm. His mother passed away in 1935, and his father followed a few years later in 1939.

At the end of '39, a new dam was being built at Possum Kingdom Lake, a reservoir of the Brazos River located in North
Texas within 100 miles of the Oklahoma border. The people in
charge of the project asked Mr. Farrow if he would leave Hill
County Electric and come oversee the building of the dam. He
went to Ft. Worth and opened an office for the Brazos River
Authority. The Possum Kingdom Dam was going to be a hydro-power plant to service part of the REA co-ops all around
that area. This would allow Hill County Electric to break away
from having to buy power from TP&L. So Mr. Farrow agreed
to work for the Brazos River Authority long enough to get the
new hydro plant up and running. While parting Itasca, Mr.
Farrow said to his right-hand man, Ralph Bailey, "I just want
one year leave of absence." So Ralph took over to manage Hill
County Electric, and Mr. Farrow uprooted and moved his family to North Texas.

"I remember the 1940s as a time when we were united in a way known only to that generation. We belonged to a common cause—the war."

— Hollywood Actress, Gene Tierney

CHAPTER FOUR

The 1940s:
The Rumblings of War

The 1940s became a time of economic boom, when the United States prepared for the possibility of entering a global war against Japan, Italy, and Nazi Germany in what would go down in history as World War II. Sixteen million American men and women joined the military, which opened up jobs for workers across the country. The economy was boosted by the production of weapons, war vehicles, boats, planes, and supplies for the war. Even women joined the workforce, working in factories as "Rosie the Riveter" and as nurses for the Red Cross.

On the rural electric front, the REA switched their efforts from building power lines to serving the war by powering the production of food for the military. In Itasca, for the first half of 1940, Manager Ralph Bailey continued to run the operations of Hill County Electric Cooperative. Linemen such as Red Hobbs and Chester Upchurch continued to build and service power lines. Meanwhile, Mr. Farrow was up in North Texas fulfilling his year of duty overseeing the construction of the Possum Kingdom Dam.

"We rented a home in Ft. Worth," recalls Gene. "Dad had an office at the dam where he could watch it being built." Mr. Farrow worked there for a year until the dam was completed. Then, in the middle of 1940, he moved his family back to Itasca and resumed his duties as manager of Hill County Electric.

Shocking News

Mr. Farrow's two boys, John Earl and Gene, worked for the Co-op doing grunt work during the summers between school semesters. Gene recalls, "I worked for . . . I think it was fifty cents an hour back then when I was in high school. I cleared right-of-way, dug post holes, strung wire, did everything a construction worker would do, no climbing. I was the grunt on the ground, running supplies from the trucks to the workers, splicing the wire together."

Mr. Farrow's oldest son, John Earl, quit college and asked to work as a lineman. His father turned him down. After what happened to Claude Cottingame, dying of electrocution a couple years back, Mr. Farrow didn't want his son working on the lines. But against his wishes, John Earl went to work as a lineman for a contractor in McGregor, Texas. Not long after, Mr. Farrow got a call that his son had been electrocuted while working on a pole and was in the hospital.

"John Earl had been burned," remembers his brother, Gene. "And he stayed alive for three days, but (the electric current) had gone through his hands and out his feet. He would have been a cripple the rest of his life had he lived, so he passed away." John Earl died in March 1940 at the age of nineteen.

Mr. Farrow was devastated and became overprotective of his youngest son, Gene, who at the time was working a summer job for the two main linemen, Red Hobbs and Chester Upchurch, digging rock holes. Mr. Farrow drove up to one of their work sites visibly upset. Gene remembers that day well, "Dad told them if he ever caught them letting me climb, he'd fire them on the spot."

As a teenager working with the linemen, Gene really wanted to climb a pole, even though it was forbidden. One time, he borrowed a lineman's spikes and climbed up a pole that wasn't hot, while Chester, Red, and the crew watched to make sure Mr. Farrow wasn't driving up the road. Gene grins, "That was their secret and mine."

Road Trips with the Farrows

Two weeks a year Earl took a vacation and the Farrow family usually went to Salisbury, North Carolina to visit his wife's sisters and brothers. Pauline came from a family of eight. Gene remembers vacationing with his father, "He would say, 'I want to leave Saturday.' So about Thursday Mom would start packing, and I'd say, 'Why are you packing so early?' She'd say, 'Son, be ready.' She'd pack up everything and sometimes on Friday about noon, Dad would say, 'Pauline, let's go ahead and go. Everything's okay, no problem. We'll leave now.' One time we left Thursday night."

Pauline always packed early because she knew Earl was

uptight all the time, and when he was ready to go someplace, they left right then. "He had nervous problems," says Gene, "because of stress or whatever you want to call it. I remember times when he'd come home for lunch. He always took a nap before he'd go back to work, and at one o'clock we'd eat lunch, and Dad would lay on the couch in the back room. He'd stay about twenty minutes or so then get up and go back to work. He had nervous, high-strung energy. He was always that way. I guess nowadays you'd call him a workaholic."

A New Source of Power

In 1941, Brazos Electric Power Cooperative was founded to generate and supply power using the hydro-power plant at the Possum Kingdom Dam. Hill County Electric finally released their shackles from TP&L and switched to buying power from Brazos Electric. Hill County Electric bought a thousand kilowatts and then sold them to the members.

Brazos Electric Power Cooperative, who provided power to all the Texas co-ops, assigned a general manager from each of the Texas co-ops to be on the board of directors. They chose Mr. Farrow to serve as president of the board.

Brazos Electric Power Cooperative, Inc.
Headquarters Facilities
Waco, Texas

America Under Attack

Throughout the year of 1941, the rumblings of war in Europe and the Pacific could be felt over here. On December 7, Japanese fighter planes bombed Pearl Harbor in Honolulu, Hawaii, destroying much of the naval fleet. Afterward, President Franklin D. Roosevelt addressed the nation, calling December 7, 1941, "a date which will live in infamy." Because of these attacks, the U.S. and its British allies declared war on Japan. By summer of 1942, a good many of the employees who worked for the cooperatives joined the military and went off to serve in the war. Mr. Farrow's assistant manager, Ralph Bailey, was one of them.

Chester Upchurch (left) and Ralph Bailey (in uniform) standing in front of the Hill County Electric truck

Wartime and the NRECA

In 1942, the Allied and Axis forces battled one another in both the Pacific and European theaters. The Allies were led by "The Big Three": the United States, Great Britain, and the Union of Soviet Socialist Republics in Russia. Other allies included Canada, Australia, New Zealand, Belgium, the Philippines, South Africa, and several others.

The Axis powers consisted of Nazi Germany, Japan, Italy, as well as Hungary, Romania, and Bulgaria. With Adolph Hitler at the helm, the Axis powers were imperializing the smaller countries in Europe, Russia, and Africa and committing atrocious war crimes.

Allied troops and tank brigades invaded North Africa and stopped the advancement of Hitler's armies. On the Eastern Front, Soviet armies held back the Germans at Stalingrad. Meanwhile, in the Pacific at the famous Battle of Midway, U.S. naval battles defeated the Imperialist Japanese Navy, causing them to retreat. The Allies celebrated a number of early victories, and while the Axis powers had stopped advancing, the war was far from over.

By 1942, the U.S. government was donating most of its manpower and resources to the war effort. This had a devastating impact on the REA. Rural electric cooperatives around the nation were under funded and suffered from being bullied by the investor-owned utility companies. The IOU lobbyists in Washington were out to destroy many of the rural electric companies. So Mr. Farrow and other advocates of rural electric co-ops went to Washington and organized the National Rural Electric Cooperative Association.

NRECA Meeting in Washington

The NRECA was set up to unite over 900 electric cooperatives that generated, transmitted, or distributed power in the U.S. The organization gave these non-profit cooperatives a solid presence in Washington and a defense against the IOU lobbyists. According to Dub Stout, "They had to fight the utility companies all along. One time a congressman was trying to set up a deal to let the power companies buy the co-op lines, but it never did go over. They just didn't get it done, because there were a lot of democratic senators up in Washington that stopped it." Mr. Farrow maintained an active presence within the NRECA.

On June 6, 1944, also known as "D-Day," Allied forces stormed the beaches of Normandy and combated German armies across France and Belgium, pushing them back all the way to their German borders. Meanwhile, in the Pacific theater, U.S. forces battled Japan with a heavy naval and air attack.

Troops fought hand-to-hand combat on islands such as Saipan, Guam, and the Philippines.

This war on two fronts continued over the next year until the Axis allies were brought to their knees. President FDR never saw the end of the war for he died on April 12, 1945, and was succeeded by President Harry S. Truman. After a global war that took countless lives, German forces surrendered to the Allies on May 7, 1945, and to the Russian army on May 8. In the Pacific, U.S. troops fought the famous battles of Iwo Jima and Okinawa and captured both islands. On August 6, the U.S. delivered a massive blow to Japan when it dropped an atomic bomb on Hiroshima. World War II finally ended in the Pacific, when Japan officially surrendered on September 2, 1945.

A New Beginning

The postwar era was a time of economic stability, as the troops came home and returned to work. Ralph Bailey got wounded in the war from shrapnel and went back to work for Hill County Electric Cooperative. Retired lineman Wesley Brackin remembers, "He come out of the service and he had worked here before, and so they had to hire him back. It was the law then. And he went in as the assistant manager." Former linemen Chester Upchurch and G.W. Cates also got out of the service. When they rejoined Hill County Electric, Chester got promoted to construction foreman and G.W. moved up to superintendent. Lineman Red Hobbs became foreman of the line crew.

In 1946, Mr. Farrow expanded his office staff and renovated the front office.

Left to Right: Faye Tippie, Ralph Bailey, Janie Ruth Barnes, Trudy Cole, Earl Farrow, and Ana Margaret Alverson

Mr. Farrow in his new office

The Whitney Lake Dam

With a new company image, Mr. Farrow set his sights on gaining larger customers, and he hit pay dirt when he won a bid to power the construction of the Whitney Lake Dam in 1946.

Gene Farrow recalls, "Dad had the contract, because we had the power all around the country out from Whitney. He furnished the power to Whitney Dam for the building of it. We used to go over there almost every day, and I can remember looking way down where they were digging it out at the bottom . . . the big hole in the ground. They had to go down to bedrock and build up. And we furnished the power for all the big equipment they had there." The Whitney Lake Dam project was a huge boon for Hill County Electric, because it brought a large, steady income into the Co-op.

With the demand to build power lines to the dam, Mr. Farrow hired more linemen. They had three crews working simultaneously. A cutting crew cleared the trees; a construction crew dug the holes and set the poles; and the linemen tied in the wire.

Wesley Brackin came on board and started working with the line crew. "I was a grunt for about seven or eight days. And what we were doing was south of Whitney. We had to clear out a right-of-way in the trees and shrubbery and stuff like that for about a mile and a half. And myself and a couple of other boys . . . we got it cleared up the way we needed it in about a week and a half." Wesley's crew then helped the construction crew dig the holes, set the poles, string the wire, and then the linemen came in and pulled the wire and tied it to the tops of the poles. "We started out going west, and it was about eight spans there . . . and we were on down to an A-4 corner . . . I'd been working maybe nine days, and that A-4 is the first pole that I climbed. I went right on up the pole and we finished the job and everything."

The Whitney Lake Dam project lasted a few years. During that time, in 1947, Dub Stout started working full-time. "I started out as a truck driver and a hole digger. It wasn't long till they put me on a pole hauler, and I hauled poles up to the linemen that had them staked. And I'd take these poles, and put one beside each of these stakes, frame it, and leave it laying there and then someone would set it and build a line on it. That's how we were able to get two miles a day."

Lineman Dub Stout

Hill County Electric's
Board of Directors

While the linemen were busy building power lines for the dam, Mr. Farrow and Ralph Bailey managed the operations, making sure that their existing members were being provided great service. Every year the members voted for new board directors to represent them. The board continued to meet regularly and made sure Mr. Farrow was running the Co-op smoothly and efficiently.

Members of the Board 1948

The Co-op's board of directors are elected by the members. The board employs the general manager which is the only employee that the board employs and terminates. The board sets the employee policies, bylaws, tariffs, which are the rates, and the requirements for membership. The manager's job is to make sure that those policies and tariffs are followed and to oversee the day to day operations. The board's main role is to make sure that the business and the policies of the cooperative are performed to the best interest of the members. So that all members are treated fairly and equally. The manager is over the Co-op's employees.

Kaboom! at the Whitney Lake Dam

The construction company building the dam was also constructing an ice plant. Wesley Brackin remembers, "We had to get electricity down there, a three-phase line, down through where the ice plant was. And this happened to be in the area of white rock, and the hole digging was going to be tough. We had four crews over there. And three men got on each hole to dig it."

At the first hole, Foreman Chester Upchurch, Manton Turner, and a third man were digging with jackhammers and got down to white rock.

"And it's really hard rock." Dub Stout remembers using an air compression trailer. "We'd drag it around and drill a hole and load that hole with dynamite. And blast that hole and then clean the rock out. That was the only way we could dig a hole."

Chester Upchurch (left) with Mr. Farrow

Wesley Brackin remembers one particular area of hard rock that was giving their jackhammers trouble. "So they took the unit off of the jackhammer and put a drill bit on it, and drilled as far as it was going to go. And Chester got a half a stick of dynamite and put it in that hole. And then he thought that wasn't going to be big enough, so he put a whole stick on top of it."

Dub says, "When they went to set it off, it wouldn't go off. It had a fuse electric cap. You stick it to a flashlight battery, anything would set it off. But this time it wouldn't do it. Why Chester did it, I'll never know. But he took the drill, put the bit into the top of that dynamite and was gonna drill it out and try to get that dynamite out of there."

Wesley says, "Chester got the jackhammer bit back under and started chipping at white rock. When he did he hit that half-stick of dynamite. And it blew up in his face."

There was a loud explosion and the jackhammer hit Chester Upchurch in the chest and dust and rock went everywhere. "His face was full of dirt," remembers Dub, "and his eyes were full of dirt. And the other men digging the holes knew something happened."

After the dust settled, Manton saw Chester was in pain and said to him, "Ah, that's gonna be all right."

Travis Farquhar and another crewman unhooked Chester from the compressor, and then Manton, who was about six-foot-six, picked up Chester and put him in his pick up. The men drove him toward Whitney. Riding between Manton and Dub, Chester said, "How am I? I can't see."

Manton said, "Oh, you don't look bad, you're okay. Just hang in there."

Chester was bleeding where rocks had hit him in the face and eyes. Manton kept telling him he looked okay. That it wasn't bad. They reached the Whitney hospital, and a doctor jumped up on the fender. He took one look at Chester, who had dirt all over him, and said, "God Almighty!"

They got him into an ambulance and delivered to a hospital in Waco. They got all the rock and dirt out of his eyes. He recovered there for a few days.

"He was okay," says Dub. "I don't know how that didn't hurt him in the chest, but the drill hit him."

Wesley laughs, "There was a time after that (Chester) could pull a rock out of his cheek, and it wouldn't bother him. He could feel that rock and he could pop it out. Anyway, he finally got them all out. He got over it."

The crew got back to work, digging holes in the white rock and installing the power lines. Not long after the dynamite incident, Chester Upchurch was back to work.

One day, Mr. Farrow arrived on the site with a serious look on his face. He had gotten wind that somebody in his crew was trying to organize the co-op employees as a union. He called his twenty men together for a meeting. Looking each man in the eye, Mr. Farrow calmly said, "Now, if y'all want to start a union, that's fine. You go right ahead. But I want you to know the day you organize a union, will be the last day that you all work for the REA. I will shut down the REA."

That speech put an end to any more talk of forming a union and it was never brought up again.

The Ice Storm of '49

"Our worst enemy in the electric industry is ice," says Gene Farrow. "Especially with the high lines. When we got an ice storm it raised havoc with a lot of the transformers. I remember this one night we had an ice storm, and all the crews were out, and sometime in the middle of the night, twelve thirty, one o'clock, it was a lot of rain just causing all kinds of outages."

Dub Stout remembers the nasty storm, "It froze everything for nearly two weeks. We lost about 500 poles. They domino two or three when they fall. The ice gets that big around on the wire. It's heavy. And when that wire breaks, the poles will jolt. We hired a contractor to come help us."

Dub and his crew went out to a substation surrounded by hills. "They were hills, but we called them mountains . . . It was

Sunday morning, and it was zero, snowing . . . That substation we had out here had a line that was going way over there, and it had flooded and the line was broken. And I climbed about a mile or mile and a half of pole, untying wire . . . and the crew came behind me to pick up the wire and stacked it. And when they got that done, I had to go back and tie them all back in."

Wesley Brackin recalls, "We found a wire down. It was sticking out the top of the pole a little past the ties. The line rotted or something. Anyhow, it fell and when it did it chopped down that line out. And I got down there and found it. And put my shoes on the pole, and like an idiot, when you have ice on a pole you climb with a belt."

"Climbing an icy pole is dangerous," says Dub. "Sometimes when you're climbing your boot hooks into the ice and not the pole and you can hit the ground pretty easy."

Wesley laughs, "Well, I went up (the pole), and that little strip of wire sticking out had some ice on it. I reached up to pull that ice off and when I did, I happened to think, well, I had my rubber gloves on but that didn't mean nothing." As an act of faith, Wesley grabbed a hold of the wire not knowing if it was alive or dead. Fortunately it was dead and he didn't get zapped. "That was the only close accident that I had in forty-four years."

Gene Farrow was a junior in high school then. And his father woke him up the first night of the storm and said, "Son, you want to go with me? I've got to go check something. We've got an outage."

All the trucks were out repairing the lines, so Mr. Farrow took it upon himself to look at one particular outage next to their sharecropping farm.

Gene said, "Sure, I'll go with you."

The Farrows had six hundred peach trees on their farm

and raised some pigs and other animals. When they got to the orchard that bordered their neighbor's fence, the road was too muddy to drive any farther.

Mr. Farrow said, "I think it's just a circuit breaker on the line. But we're going to have to walk part of the way."

Gene remembers, "We got out of the car. I got part of this pole and he got part, and we had a flashlight. And we had to walk, it seemed like about a half mile, down this muddy road at night. And it was just as dark as pitch going all the way down. And he got to the pole and he looked up and said, 'Yeah, the switch is wrong.'"

Using the two thin metal poles they brought, they assembled a long shovel-like tool with an extension on it. Put together, it was about thirty feet long. Mr. Farrow reached the pole up to the transformer's junction box, pulled on it, and reset it.

Gene says, "I remember turning around and starting to walk back and the power was on at the house, because they had probably gone out while they were sitting up and . . . didn't turn their lights out. You could see the lights on then as we headed back to the car."

Dub says, "Next morning, in the office, the foreman told them I had fixed all those poles the day before, and Mr. Farrow said, 'Well, let's give him a nickel raise.' That was really good . . . back in those days we were making sixty-five to seventy cents an hour. I think the nickel gave me seventy cents an hour."

With the help of a contracting crew, it took the linemen two weeks to fix the 500 poles that were down, but the ice finally thawed, and they got the power back up and running to the rural homes and businesses.

By the end of the 1940s, Harry S. Truman was still president. And while Americans had been united through patriotism after the victory of World War II, the U.S. entered a new Cold War with the Soviet Union, which brought on fears of espionage and the spread of communism.

In the little town of Itasca, Texas, Mr. Farrow and his employees kept their focus on servicing their members and building close to two miles of power line a day.

"Against the dark background of the atomic bomb, the United States does not wish merely to present strength, but also the desire and the hope for peace."

— President Dwight D. Eisenhower
at the United Nations
December 8, 1953

CHAPTER FIVE

The 1950s:
Steady Growth

The 1950s were characterized by the Cold War with the Soviets, McCarthyism, the Korean War, and the emergence of Rock n' Roll. Legendary stars like Elvis Presley and Jerry Lee Lewis sang and played music with a passion that had teens going wild. The television set became common in households, and popular shows were *I Love Lucy*, *Father Knows Best*, and *The Ed Sullivan Show*.

Hill County Electric Cooperative maintained stability and positive growth. Mr. Farrow continued to deliver power not only to the rural people, but also influenced the electric cooperative industry as a whole. He made several trips to Washington. Heavily active with the NRECA, he served for two years as Vice President.

Gene Farrow remembers, "They had a meeting of the REA co-ops nationwide once a year. And they were almost always in the beginning out of Washington. Later on I know he and sometimes Claude Wakefield and C.W. Johns would go with him. And what he would do is drive to Salisbury, North Carolina, leave Mother and I there, and take the train up to Washington, go to his meeting, then pick us up and take us home."

Helping LBJ

Lyndon B. Johnson was a big supporter of the REA. He lived in Pedernales, Texas and pushed getting the Pedernales Co-op up and running. He was also friends with Mr. Farrow.

Gene remembers, "I guess I was in high school at the time, in the summer, and (Dad) said, 'Do you want to go with me up to Washington?' So I went with him and we had one luncheon with Lyndon Johnson. He was Senator then."

Later, when LBJ was in Dallas and running for a second term with the Senate, he called Mr. Farrow and asked him to introduce him at a rally in Hillsboro. Gene says about his father, "So he went down to Hillsboro to the political rally and introduced Lyndon Johnson to the crowd."

An Achievement in Safety

After losing Claude Cottingame to electrocution back in the late 1930s, Mr. Farrow took great pride in making sure his crews were practicing safety while they worked with the power lines. This earned Hill County Electric a Safety Award for going a consecutive number of days without an accident.

Safety Award Presentation

Annual Member Meetings

Every year Hill County Electric hosts annual meetings for its members. Gene remembers the first meetings, "We used to have them all in Itasca. We used the gymnasium in the high school for the meeting for all the people to come. And they'd have a barbecue and give away appliances as door prizes. And they'd have an election and Dad would make a speech for different people and about the progress of the Co-op, and then they would elect the board."

Member meeting at Itasca's high school gym

Later, as the membership grew too big for the gym, the annual meetings were moved out to the high school football field.

Member meeting on the high school football field

Three Miles a Day

The late 1950s became a time for expansion and building more power lines across the rural regions.

Wesley Brackin recalls, "In '57 Mr. Farrow got the notice from the big shots up there (in Washington), and we had to build three miles of line a day. And everybody would be on the job. That's what we'd be working for."

The crews didn't always build toward somebody's house or business. There were many days they built lines out in the country with no particular destination. Wesley remembers their instructions were to "just go out there and find a place we could build that much line that day. Chester would go out there ahead of us and find something to do, and that's where we'd start, trying to get in three miles a day. If it was muddy or raining, we still had to stay on it. Of course, the company here was run on government money then. In other words they had to borrow so much money to operate and they had to borrow it through the REA in Washington. And they had to borrow enough money to build three miles of line, because it took ten thousand dollars to build three miles of line, and they'd say we're going to build ten of it, thirty miles."

No matter how fast the crews worked, they had difficulty meeting the demands of Washington. Wesley says, "Three miles, it would probably take us three days. Because we had one crew digging the hole. Another crew would come along and set the poles and tamp them in. A wire crew stringing the wire out. And then here comes the linemen, putting it up."

Trucks & Diggers

By 1958, Mr. Farrow had forty-eight linemen working on his crews. With the need to work at a faster pace, he invested in some new construction equipment. They had a few wench trucks but their digging machine was out of date. Wesley remembers, "Back then we had an old hole digger, and to set the poles they had a great big old Army truck called "The FWD."

Dub Stout recalls, "It was a World War I Army truck. It

had FWD wrote on (the side.) You had to climb a ladder to get up to it. I don't know what the FWD stood for. It was the company's first digger truck."

"And it had the boom on it," says Wesley Brackin. "And that's the only thing we had to work with."

The crew asked Ralph Bailey why they kept using it and he responded, "While that old truck is out of date and all that, it's about the only one that can drive."

Mr. Farrow stayed in contact with his line crews using a radio that was set up back at headquarters. He got wind of the crew complaining that their trucks were slowing them down, so he brought in a new digger. And then bought a new pole truck.

"That was when we really started going," remembers Wesley. "We started hiring, in that year we had forty-eight men out in the field. I mean anybody who wanted to work out there, they put them on, coming and going."

Hill County Electric Cooperative staff and board members

By the end of the 1950s, Dwight D. "Ike" Eisenhower was still president. While the Korean War was over, having ended in 1953, the Cold War with the Soviet Union was still keeping Americans in fear of the spread of communism and a nuclear war. Drive-in movie screens featured sci-fi movies like *Invasion from Mars* and *Them*, a movie about atomic red ants attacking civilization. In 1959, a new threat emerged very close to home as Fidel Castro established a communist government in Cuba and became allies with the Soviets. The simple days of the 1950s were falling away as America entered a period of chaos in the 1960s.

"We choose to go to the moon in this decade and do the other things, not because they are easy, but because they are hard, because that goal will serve to organize and measure the best of our energies and skills, because that challenge is one that we are willing to accept, one we are unwilling to postpone, and one which we intend to win, and the others, too."

— President John F. Kennedy
"Moon Speech" at Rice University
Summer 1962

CHAPTER SIX

The 1960s:
Reaching for the Moon

The Sixties began as a decade of radical change, as John F. Kennedy became president and spoke with high ideals of civil rights, social reforms, and building a space program that would land the first man on the moon. The Cold War between the U.S. and the Soviets was ratcheting up tension between the world's two superpowers. And the potential of a new war was brewing as military advisors were sent to recon a growing force of guerillas in a little country called Vietnam.

Meanwhile, Hill County Electric, still under the leadership of Earl Farrow, was going through a few changes of its own. The success of a growing membership and building power lines for clients like the Whitney Dam gave the Cooperative the resources to expand. In 1961, they remodeled the main office.

Two clerks working in the newly renovated main office

Mr. Farrow speaking at a Director's Board Meeting in 1961

The financial success also allowed the Cooperative to pay down its debts. On May 3, 1962, Hill County Electric paid off the last of its REA loan in the amount of $306,632. This monumental moment put them in the black and from here on out, the Cooperative could continue to grow from its own revenues.

Mr. Farrow handing a final check to the REA

VOUCHER CHECK			N?	2106

HILL COUNTY ELECTRIC COOPERATIVE, INC.

Payment in full on following REA Notes, as of May 9, 1962:

Account No.	Principal	Current Interest	Acct. No.	
(4010) #224.2A	$ 105,630.07			
(4020) .231	65,791.86			
(4030) .201	54,476.41			
(4040) .201	20,205.04			
(4050) .281	20,597.91			
(4060) .282	38,674.74			
	$ 305,460.03	$ 1,171.97	#237.1	306,632.00

GENERAL FUND   N? 2106

HILL COUNTY ELECTRIC COOPERATIVE, INC.

Payment in full on REA Notes #4010, 20, 30, 40, 50 & 60 as of May 9, 1962

$ 306,632.00

To THE FIRST NATIONAL BANK OF ITASCA
ITASCA, TEXAS   May 3, 1962

PAY Three Hundred Six Thousand Six Hundred Thirty-Two and no/100 - - - - - - - DOLLARS

TO THE ORDER OF

Rural Electrification Administration

"Dad was very proud of the day," remembers Gene Farrow. "They made a big hubbub about paying off their loan. For several years they had borrowed money based on their needs from the government. And Hill County Electric was on their own. They were in the black."

The Upchurch Brothers

At Hill County Electric, a new generation of young linemen began working on the force, as high school boys worked summers and started full time once they graduated. It was very common for the boys of Itasca to follow in their father's footsteps and come to work for Mr. Farrow. Chester Upchurch's two boys, Kenneth and Ronnie, began working the brush crews for their dad.

Kenneth Upchurch recalls, "I went to work with Dad, both of us did, every opportunity we got. And they were building out across the pasture, across some ditches and stuff and they couldn't drive a truck to pull the wire out. So they were having to pull it out by hand. So I just jumped off the truck and started grabbing the wire and helping the guys pull the wire out. I was just out there, I wasn't employed or anything. And Mr. Farrow drove up. And that afternoon we started home, and Dad said, 'How'd you like to work here every day?' And I said, 'Man, I'd love it.' And he said, 'Well, Mr. Farrow said you can start tomorrow.' So I worked here the summer of my eighth grade year. And I worked here every summer until I retired."

Kenneth fondly calls his brother, Ronnie, by his nickname "Rock." "Rock and I would go work with our Dad. We would get in his truck on Sunday afternoon, and get his tools out. We'd climb clothesline poles. We climbed trees. We climbed everything."

Ronnie Upchurch says, "I can't ever remember when I couldn't put Dad's tools on and climb a pole. And I never cared about doing anything else. That's all I ever wanted to do was be a lineman."

Kenneth says, "In the summers, when Rock was in high school, they had a brush crew here. Our boss was Buster Partlow. We had an axe and a saw and he'd go out and show us what he wanted us to cut. And we'd cut."

"And get wasp-stung," laughs Ronnie. "Golly boom, I'd come in the evening and my eyes would be swelled up I couldn't even see. But, gosh, we was bringing in a dollar an hour. That was eight dollars a day. And we went in the pickup. Buster drove and Mike Vincent rode in the front. And me and Gene Hooper climbed in the back. We rode to West in the back of the truck. Enjoyed every bit of it."

"And I worked in the construction crew," says Kenneth. "And Mr. Farrow's nephew, he worked in the construction crew, as well. His name was Jerry McMahan. Another man, Manton Turner, he worked in the service crew and they hired his son, and he worked in the construction crew. They were excellent people and let the kids work here in the summer time. And that was the dream of every kid in town was to get to work here in the summer time, because of the people who were here. They were fun to be around. It wasn't at all like a job. It was more like a play day to be with these guys."

When the Upchurch brothers were working here, the boys working the crew horsed around a lot. One time they were building a three-phase line near a large packing feed lot. Ronnie Upchurch and all the brush-crew boys were clearing out trees and tamping poles. At quitting time, Rex Turner, who drove the winch truck, and Dickie Meyers, who drove the digger, decided to race back to the headquarters, because the road was dusty and it was too hot to roll the windows up, so whoever was in the rear got a face full of dust.

Kenneth remembers, "Rex jumped into the winch truck and Dickie jumped into the dig machine, and one of them wanted to get in front of the other before they got to that dusty road. Rex wheels this A-frame truck around and it had two bolts at the top. Well, he hung one of these guys and I mean it broke that pole off just as smooth as a whistle at about twelve foot."

So the crew went back to headquarters and Rex confessed to their foreman, Chester Upchurch, "I broke that pole off."

And Chester said, "What pole?"

Rex said, "That pole we just set."

"How'd you do that?"

"Me and Dickie were racing and I hung it with that A-frame and broke it."

And Chester said, "You ain't gonna have much check left, are you?" And Rex said, "No, sir, but that's what happened." The brush-crew boys all had a good laugh at Rex's expense.

Like Father, Like Sons

In the early days, the line crews used dynamite when their digger couldn't break up the hard rock. It was Kenneth and Ronnie Upchurch's father, Chester, who first had the mishap when a stick of dynamite blew rock into his face and he had to be rushed to the hospital. Years later, Kenneth and Ronnie got their own chance to work with dynamite.

Kenneth recalls working at one site and trying to break up the rock. "They had a drill, and they'd drill that hole and put dynamite in it. And then we'd all back off and we had about a hundred-foot shooting cord. And you'd tie that cord, and everybody would go back and get behind trucks or trees, and they'd shoot that thing off. And get under something, because the rocks are gonna come down from everywhere. And there was an old gentleman who had a tree in his front yard. And he had been trying to pull that tree up with a tractor. He finally cut it off and he just had a stump there."

The man noticed the linemen using dynamite and asked them, "Could y'all put some of that under that stump?"

And Kenneth said, "We could put a half a stick under there and blow it up for you."

Ronnie remembers the old man and his battle with the stump. "We had about a nine-foot crowbar that they used to dig holes by hand. Well, they just took that crow bar and just went to working it up and down, and actually, they don't know how much dynamite they put under there. Well, there were some old bricks that was covered up that they didn't even know was there. And when they shot the dynamite, it just blowed the stump plumb out of the ground. And those bricks, some of them wound up on top of his house. And he come walking back up there and my daddy-in-law told him, 'My God, it's amazing what a half stick of dynamite can do.' And there's no telling how much dynamite they had in there."

Both Kenneth and Ronnie laugh, remembering the look on that old man's face at the sight of all the bricks on his roof. Eventually, Hill County Electric got a more powerful digger and discontinued using dynamite.

Kenneth says, "They had a digging machine back when Mr. Farrow was manager. But something happened because of the old truck, and they didn't have enough money to get a new truck. So they took the digging machine off of that old truck and put it in the alley back here and set it up on some barrels. For years it stayed there and they dug all the holes by hand.

And then they got a digger. It was a fixed digger, in other words, it wasn't a wiggle-tail digger. You had to back the truck up until you got it on the spot. And then they got one that would turn. The bit, you could rotate the turn. And all of this was improvements, of course."

The linemen getting a re-closure demonstration for training. The only man not wearing a hat is Kenneth Upchurch.

The New Kid

In the summer of 1962, another long-standing employee, William Watson, was working with his dad building a fence and it was a very hot day. They had forgotten to bring water and were growing thirsty. They noticed a tree-cutting crew working nearby.

"They were at the tailgate drinking water," William Watson remembers, "so I walked off up there and asked them for a drink of water. And talked to them a little bit. And the man that was supervising the crew, Buster Partlow, asked me what I was gonna do for the summer. I said, 'Well, when I get this job finished today I'm gonna be waiting on another job.' So the next day he rode up into the yard where I lived and asked me if I wanna go to work for him. I said, 'Okay.'"

On the following Monday, William went to the office and filled out the paperwork and Mr. Farrow asked for his social security number.

William said, "I don't have a social security number."

Mr. Farrow said, "Well, you have to have one." He escorted William down to the post office and got him fixed up with a social security number. William remembers fondly of Mr. Farrow, "He was running the whole show, but he wasn't too busy to take care of the minor details."

Employee Picnics

Every year in July Mr. Farrow and his wife, Pauline, hosted a picnic just for the employees. The Farrows lived a couple of blocks from the main office. "They had a house down here on Adam's Street," remembers Dub Stout. "We had the 'Annual Picnic,' they called it." Mr. and Mrs. Farrow hosted the picnics in their own backyard. And a neighbor by the name of Columbus Johnson barbecued chicken in an old screened-in hut. Ronnie Upchurch recalls, "The week of the barbecue, you might as well get ready to load up a truck load of wood and bring it to Columbus where he'd have wood to cook barbecue with. It was very exciting to go up there and just eat, because Columbus could cook barbecued chicken. Mr. Farrow used to get upset because he'd tell Columbus to make the barbecue sauce hot, and Columbus never could make it hot enough."

William Watson says, "Yeah, he cooked them chickens down in the flat and we went down there and picked them up."

Dub says, "And when the chicken was about ready, Chester Upchurch would go get the chicken about time, put 'em in a big dish pan, these half chickens. And it was the best barbecue chicken you ever ate in your life."

Mr. Farrow's wife, Pauline, was the one in charge. According to her son, Gene, "She ran the picnics. She was the social."

Bob Wilson says, "The ladies, actually the moms, would get together and go into Mr. Farrow's house and they would make the fixin's to go with it. And back then, they never had dessert like a cake or pie. They always bought ice cream on a stick."

Dub smiles as he remembers, "Mr. Farrow would always bring out the ice cream on a stick and pass them around. There was a lot of people there. All the employees and their wives. They didn't have the kids come or otherwise it would have been too many."

Kenneth Upchurch says, "It was a fun deal to go to, because again, of the type of people who worked here."

Mr. Farrow and his wife, Pauline

As the Cooperative's social organizer, Pauline Farrow also hosted the Christmas parties every year, as well as the member meetings. Gene remembers about his mother, "She didn't get involved with the workings of the REA. She was not a paid employee. She was in charge of the Christmas parties they always had. She ran those. She was kind of the mother hen of the REA and helped organize the barbecues of the members' (meetings). She was a full partner with him."

The Christmas parties were held at the main office. In the beginning, it was tradition for the employees to exchange gifts. They got together as one big happy family.

The Wife of a Lineman

Back in the Sixties, one of the biggest challenges the wife of a lineman faced was that for one week a month he was on call twenty-four hours a day in case a power line went out. Hill County Electric didn't have a dispatch then, so when there was an outage, the members called directly to the houses of the linemen.

Rose Marie Brackin remembers when her husband, Wesley, worked as a lineman. "For years, when he went on call, I was on call for seven days a week. I was expected to stay right by the phone. And if he had a line out and he was out on it, and two or three more lines went out, it was up to me to call other trucks in and get them out to other outages."

Wesley Brackin says, "She had no way of calling us on the job. She had a list of names and we wouldn't know whether or not we had them back home."

Rose Marie says, "They started out calling us on our phone. And finally they put the Hill County Electric phone in our home. And they expect us, for no pay mind you . . . you don't know how hard it was. I mean, outages, outages. I remember one time having five trucks out and people were calling in constantly. You would no more than hang up until another one would call. And that went on and on until they got all those lines on and he came in." Rose Marie laughs, "It was really a full-time job. And it was hard when you got two little boys and one's a baby and the other's five years old. We were told the phone comes first, the kids can cry."

Kenneth Upchurch recalls, "If it was Dad's time to answer the phone, and the phone rang, Dad would leave and go on the outage. My mother would answer that phone. And then she would call all the other guys to go to work. Like she'd call Rock. 'Can you go to work? I've got an outage here.' She didn't line up or organize anything, she just got people out. And she'd fight that thing, and if it got real big, she'd call Ralph or whoever the manager might be and tell them, and then they would come to the office. She'd been up at all hours of the night making phone calls."

Ronnie Upchurch's wife, Linda, also had to handle calls. "When I started going on call in 1965, my wife went on call, too. She worked over at the bank. Like when I'd leave, she'd answer the phone. I might answer the phone for a week and it might not ring two or three times, and then it was somebody out of lights. And then they started collecting. Going out and collecting and taking people's meters out. If you were on call, they'd say, 'Here's the disconnect list, you need to go set these three meters back.' Well, I'd take that list to our house and I'd give it to Linda. When people called in with their meter took out, they wanted to talk to somebody that could tell them about their bill. I mean, they didn't want to talk to a woman that worked at the bank, but that's just the way they did it. It got to where it was just a hassle."

Ronnie remembers, "I got in one day and the receiver on the phone was laying off the hook. And I told Linda, 'What's going on?' And she said, 'I'm tired of the man cussing me out and so I took it off the hook.' And so I put it back on the hook. Well, it hadn't been on there thirty seconds till it rang and this guy screamed at me and I just laid the sun of a gun down, walked over and sat down, went back over in a minute, picked it up. He was saying, 'Hello? Hello?' And I told him, 'You're not talking to my wife. You're talking to me. And if you want to holler and scream like an idiot, I'm fixin' to lay her down again.' And so I had to wind up setting his meter, and he was going to kick everybody's butt at Hill County Electric, and he was going to do this and he was going to do that. Well, when I got up to his house, he sent his little girl out with the money, and he wouldn't even come out of the house. And it got down to the point where all the women were like that. And they finally just told them, 'We aren't going to answer no more.'"

The linemen and their wives still handled the calls for several more years until a dispatch system was set up at the main headquarters.

Anger Management

Often times, when the linemen had to make house calls to collect money or turn off power that was being used illegally, they had to deal with angry homeowners. One day, Ronnie Upchurch got a call from the office to go set a meter back. The customer was way overdue on his electric bill. The dispatcher warned Ronnie, "Rock, this guy is mad. I'm telling you, he is mad, so I'm sending Paul Walters to go with you. Now watch this guy."

On the drive up to the delinquent customer's house, Paul shared with Ronnie his theory on how to deal with angry customers. Paul said, "Now, Rock, just watch how I handle him."

When they pulled up to the yard, the man stormed out the front door, shouting, "I'm gonna tell you ..."

Paul lurched out of the pickup and slammed the door. "You ain't gonna tell me nothing! I'm fixin' to tell you something! If you want that meter in that socket you get in the house and get me the money."

The man just froze.

Paul glared. "You stand there and looking at me ain't gonna get this meter in that socket. I said get me the money!"

The man said, "Well, I-I got my checkbook. Will you take a check?"

"I will if it's good," Paul snapped back. "If it ain't no good, we're going through this whole thing again when they disconnect you for a hot check."

The man walked over to the truck and wrote him a check. As Paul was writing out the receipt, the man said, "Sir, I don't need a receipt. I have a blank check."

"I don't care if you need it or not. You're gonna get it." Paul then told Ronnie, "Go set that meter."

"Yes, sir." Ronnie walked over and set the meter.

The homeowner said, "I-I-I certainly appreciate y'all coming up here."

"You're welcome!" Paul growled as he got in the truck and slammed the door.

They were about a half mile down the road, when Paul started laughing. He asked Ronnie, "You think that guy was *mad*?"

Ronnie said, "When he come out of that house, he looked like to me he was mad."

Paul said, "How'd you like to live in a big house like that with two or three automobiles sitting around there and get your lights cut off for a hundred dollars? That guy ain't mad. He's embarrassed."

Paul Walters had a theory on how to manage hostile customers: act madder than them and that will diffuse them quickly.

Times They Are a-Changin'

By the mid '60s, as the war in Vietnam heated up, anti-war rallies brought about strife and restlessness at home. In 1964, the Beatles played on *The Ed Sullivan Show*, launching what would be known as the "British Invasion," as bands like The Rolling Stones and The Who quickly followed. Their long hair was one of the catalysts for men of the younger generation growing their hair long and starting the Hippy Movement. Fashion changed dramatically, as people wore rebelliously loud colors, bell-bottomed jeans, and tie-dye tee-shirts with peace signs. Women exposed their bodies by wearing bikinis, mini-skirts, and go-go boots. Singers like Bob Dylan sang about how the times were changing. And in 1966, after watching police brutally beating protestors, Buffalo Springfield released the song "For What It's Worth," singing that "Something's happening here. What it is ain't exactly clear."

As change was happening all across the nation, Mr. Farrow did his best to keep the culture of Hill County Electric in line with the original values he had established from the beginning.

William Watson remembers how the radical Sixties influenced the linemen. "There was a little beard growing contest going on, and Mr. Farrow told one of the young men that we didn't need any beatniks working here at Hill County Electric. That was the terminology for them back then. It went from beatniks to hippies."

Member Picnics of the Sixties

Hill Country Electric continued their tradition of holding annual picnics for the members at the high school football field in Itasca. Here, members voted on who would represent them on the board of directors.

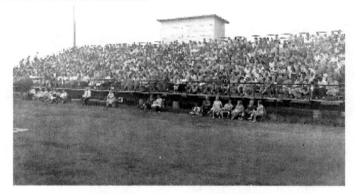

Itasca High School Football Field

Ladies preparing food for the picnic

As an incentive for people to attend the picnics, the Co-op held a drawing and appliances were given away as door prizes.

Members checking out the door prizes

Raffle drawing

A family posing after winning a TV

The crowd enjoying the evenings entertainment

The Kingfish of Itasca

By the late Sixties, Mr. Farrow was still the operating manager. Even though the Co-op's board of directors had the power to hire a new manager, there was no one more worthy to manage Hill County Electric Cooperative than its beloved founder. He was involved with every facet of the business from answering to all his employees to meeting face to face with members.

Mr. Farrow, whose nickname had been "Kingfish" among the crew, had a boat, and he and Ralph loved to go fishing.

In 1967, Mr. Farrow received a plaque in San Francisco for 25 years of service to the NRECA. He was recognized as one of the "Great Pioneers" of the Rural Electric Cooperative Program.

EARL B. H. FARROW . . . TALENTED LEADERSHIP   —Item Staff Photo.

E. D. H. Farrow Honored San Francisco As One 'Great Pioneers' REC Program

E. D. H. Farrow, Manager of Hill County Electric Cooperative, Inc., was honored at the fifth General Session of the 20th Annual Meeting of National Rural Electric Cooperative Association in San Francisco last week.

Registering at the meeting were 8,833 persons from over the United States.

President Paul H. Tidwell presented Mr. Farrow with a plaque in honor of his 25 years of service to rural electrification.

The plaque, engraved on silver, reads as follows:

"E. D. H. Farrow stands forth as one of the great pioneers in organizing the strength of the rural electric cooperative program.

"Starting with the organization of Hill County Electric Cooperative at Itasca, Texas, which he has served as manager since that time, Mr. Farrow has demonstrated talented leadership as an organizer and incorporator of Brazos Electric Power Cooperative, as an organizer of Texas Electric Cooperatives, and as incorporator and member of the First Board of Directors of the National Rural Electric Cooperative Association.

"In recognition of his lengthy and effective service, and as the single remaining incorporator of National Rural Electric Cooperative Association still actively engaged in our program, this Silver Anniversary Citation is presented by the Board of Directors on behalf of the membership at the 20th Annual Membership Meeting in San Francisco, California, on February 23, 1967."

In response Mr. Farrow effectively told of the beginning of National Rural Electric Cooperative Association in Cincinnati, Ohio and how the organization was later moved to Washington, D. C. He expressed continuing support of the NRECA program and the future of rural America.

Present from Itasca to proudly observe the presentation to Mr. Farrow were Mrs. Farrow, Ralph Bailey, Elmo Hooper, Mrs. Lucille Coffey and Mrs. Mary Westbrook.

The group returned to Itasca on Sunday morning, February 26.

The Farrow Room

In 1968, Earl Farrow was nearing retirement. To honor Mr. and Mrs. Farrow for their community services in the electric field and their church, long-time friend and contractor, A.G. Ainsworth, funded the building of the Farrow Room.

Dub Stout remembers, "Before it became the Farrow Room, it was a warehouse. A place to keep the old trucks. They moved the warehouse and made the Farrow Room out of that warehouse."

Earl and Pauline with A.G. and Alice Ainsworth

THE

BOARD OF DIRECTORS

OF

HILL COUNTY ELECTRIC COOPERATIVE, INC.

AND

A. G. and ALICE AINSWORTH

Cordially Invites You To
Attend The Dedication Of

The Farrow Room

HONORING EARL and PAULINE FARROW
111 MAIN STREET, ITASCA, TEXAS
SUNDAY, AUGUST 18, 1968, AT 3:00 P.M.

Foyer to the Farrow Room

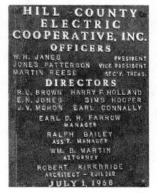

HILL COUNTY
ELECTRIC
COOPERATIVE, INC.
OFFICERS
W. H. JANES   PRESIDENT
JONES PATTERSON   VICE PRESIDENT
MARTIN REESE   SEC'Y. TREAS.
DIRECTORS
R. C. BROWN   HARRY F. HOLLAND
E. N. JONES   SIMS HOOPER
J. V. MOHON   EARL CONNALLY
EARL D. H. FARROW
MANAGER
RALPH BAILEY
ASS'T. MANAGER
WM. B. MARTIN
ATTORNEY
ROBERT KIRKBRIDE
ARCHITECT — BUILDER
JULY 1, 1968

Second plaque in the foyer

The Farrow Room was built for the Cooperative to use for meetings and other social events, like family reunions, baby showers, and retirement parties.

The Farrow Room just before the Open House

Mrs. Dorothy Moore hugging Pauline Farrow

Guests visiting at the celebration

A.G. Ainsworth giving a speech at the open house

Miss Deena Patton, Mrs. Kay Patton, and Miss Amanda Upchurch
singing a personalized version of "Dear Hearts and Gentle People"

Mr. Farrow expressing his gratitude

Farewell to an American Icon

Just three months after the celebration of the Farrow Room, in November of 1968, a mournful day came to the family at Hill County Electric Cooperative as Mr. Farrow passed away from cancer. He was 73. He accomplished much during his lifetime. He paved the roads of Itasca, sold furniture, worked as a mortician, and served as deacon at his church and mayor of the town. He married the "Cookie Girl" he fell in love with, Pauline, and together they raised two boys, John Earl and Billy Gene. Back when farmers didn't have power, Earl Farrow saw his dream of bringing power to the rural people come to fruition. He managed Hill County Electric Cooperative from its inception in 1937 until 1968. He was a pioneer not just for the five counties he delivered power to, but also for rural electric cooperatives across the nation. He helped found the NRECA and acted as vice president for two years. He oversaw the construction of the Possum Kingdom Dam, and served as president of the board for Brazos Electric Cooperative. He provided jobs to many of the men and women in Itasca, and started a power company that boosted the town's economy.

"He was as confident as they come," remembers Dub Stout. "If you ever just wanted to talk to him, he'd talk to you . . . what he meant is what he said. He never puffed up just to make it look good. He just told the truth, and he was a very honest person."

Before his death, Mr. Farrow had one final request. Ronnie Upchurch recalls a story his father, Chester, told him.

"Daddy was sitting up there in the office one time, and Mr. Farrow told him, 'Come here. I want to show you something.' So they walked into the Farrow Room, and he told Daddy, 'When I die, I want my casket laid right here.' They had his funeral at the Presbyterian Church, but they had his body in the Farrow Room." And that's where they held his memorial ceremony.

Earl D. H. Farrow was an icon who touched the lives of many. He would be missed, but always remembered.

In loving memory of Earl D. H. Farrow (1895-1968)

Three Generations: Earl Farrow with son, Billy Gene, and grandson, Martin Devon

A New Leader for a New Era

Ralph Bailey (Manager 1968-1976)

After Mr. Farrow passed away, his second in command, Ralph Bailey, took over as Manager.

Ronnie Upchurch remembers what it was like having his uncle running the Co-op. "When Uncle Ralph became the manager, my philosophy didn't change one bit, because when I started I worked for my dad (Chester). My dad was the crew foreman and I was in his crew. I just more or less told myself that I wasn't going to do anything or get caught in any situation that would embarrass Daddy. And that was the theory I had. And then when Uncle Ralph became the manager, a lot of stuff didn't change."

Kenneth agrees with his brother about their uncle. "We were both very close to Ralph, because he was, of course, Mom's brother, and they had no children. And Rock and my sister, Amanda, and I, we were basically their kids."

Ronnie remembers his uncle was funny when it came to his hobbies. "Uncle Ralph got into collecting knives and guns and watches. Stuff like that. Well, I don't guess at any time in his life he had over two dollars cash on him, but he always had his checkbook. If he saw a knife he wanted he'd just write a check for it. Well, he had his bank statements sent to the Co-op. And he'd go through the bank statements, and the checks he didn't want his wife to see, he'd take them out. And I told him one time, 'Now, Uncle Ralph that ain't gonna work. When BooBoo adds all that up, it's not going to add up.' Ralph had said, 'Ah, she don't pay no attention to that.' And stuff he didn't want her to see, he'd take those checks out and hide from her.

"They bought them a brand new car one time. A Buick. They had it about a week, and he went to a funeral right here at the cemetery, and he drove over a curb and it bent the fender on that car. And we told him, 'Uncle Ralph? Are you going to have that fixed?' And Ralph said, "Nah, BooBoo will never notice that.'"

For the most part, Ralph Bailey maintained the company's family culture that had been set in place by Mr. Farrow. The biggest change Ralph made was he gave the organization more structure. At the next board meeting he recommended to the board that the Co-op needed an Assistant General Manager of Operations. The board agreed, and Ralph awarded the position to his brother-in-law, Chester Upchurch. He also created the position of Superintendent, and promoted G.W. Cates to fulfill that role. With the new hierarchy, employees no longer answered directly to just the General Manager, and Ralph was more able to delegate some of the leadership tasks of a cooperative that was continuing to grow.

The 1960s was a time of change, revolution, and political setbacks. The nation witnessed the assassination of their country's leader, when President John F. Kennedy was assassinated in Dallas in November 1963. His brother Bobby Kennedy was later assassinated in 1968. Civil Rights activist Dr. Martin Luther King, Jr. was shot and killed that same year. The American people witnessed violence on TV. They watched their sons and brothers, husbands and friends go off to fight a war in Vietnam, while anti-war protestors rallied for peace at home.

The music industry had a huge influence on the younger generation's politics, as dozens of musicians like Jimi Hendrix, Janis Joplin, and the Grateful Dead played for a monumental outdoor music festival at Woodstock. As President Lyndon B. Johnson finished his term, Richard Nixon, holding up double-peace signs, took over as President in January, 1969. And as JFK promised at the beginning of the decade, man indeed landed on the moon during the Apollo 11 mission on July, 20, 1969.

"May the Force be with you."

— from the movie *Star Wars*
1977

CHAPTER SEVEN

The 1970s:
A New Generation

The tumultuous times of the 1960s continued into the first half of the 1970s. Political activists marched for civil rights, women's rights, environmental protection, and ending the Vietnam War. The nation's leadership came under fire due to the Watergate Scandal—a Republican plot to break into the Democratic National Committee headquarters. After being linked to the political scandal President Richard Nixon resigned in 1974 and Vice President Gerald Ford took over. The Vietnam War finally ended in 1975. Americans, ready to let loose and have fun, returned to a time of recreation. Pop culture was heavily influenced by art, literature, music, movies, and fashion. Both men and women wore bell-bottom jeans and kept their hair long. The mini skirt was still in fashion and platform shoes were introduced. Men wore three-piece leisure suits and women wore jumpsuits. The music of the Bee Gees spawned the trend of Disco dancing at nightclubs. And movies like *Saturday Night Fever, Jaws,* and *Star Wars* topped the box office.

For Hill County Electric Cooperative, the Seventies marked a time of positive growth, the implementation of new technologies, and the expansion of their work force. A new generation of linemen came on board. David "Buck" Brackin, like so many boys growing up in Itasca, followed in the footsteps of his father, Wesley Brackin. "You know like a lot of people, they follow what their dad does," says David. "I just thought it was interesting I knew back then that electricity will be here tomorrow, pretty stable. And I worked with him some. When I got here I started working with different people. It was just in my blood, and I enjoyed it."

In 1971, Milton Cranfill, Gene Farquhar, Tommy Cox, and Gary "Shorty" Lewis also joined the force. The top pay at that time for an incoming employee was two dollars an hour. Tommy Cox recalls, "I got started July the 1st in '71. So I had me what some people called a permanent job drawing two dollars an hour. I always wanted a steady job before I got married, so I got married July the 2nd. Dub Stout was my foreman . . . and Dub looked at me and said, 'T.C., if I was you, if I was getting married tonight, and it was my second day . . . I believe I would go on to the house.' It was pretty neat. Second day on the job, and they let you go home early. I appreciated that."

Milton Cranfill remembers, "I went to college a year and a half and decided the Vietnam War was going. I joined the Army Reserves and quit school. Because when you quit school it took about three weeks for me to get my induction notice. If you were not already in a branch of the service, you were going to Vietnam. I joined the Reserves and came to work at Hill County Electric.

"I'll never forget the first day," Milton continues. "I built a line off Fort Graham Road right out from Ross . . . Not knowing a lot, first thing we learned how to do was how to ground poles. Well, I could handle a hammer. And I helped ground those poles and come to find out about 1-1:30 that afternoon, I was telling my brother-in-law, Ronnie (Upchurch), 'My arms are burning up.' Come to find out there's such a thing called Creosote. And I had it splattered all over me. That's how the poles are treated. As I was driving the poles into the ground, I was hitting them a little excessive, and the hammer head hitting the pole was splattering this Creosote. You don't see it … And it was burning me pretty good. I felt like someone was holding a torch up to me."

Cat Climbing and Burning Poles

One of the requirements of working the lineman's job is climbing the wood poles. Larry Farquhar describes his first time on a pole, "It was kind of like a pig trying to walk on ice. It wasn't very pretty and was plenty scary."

David Brackin remembers watching his dad climb, "We called it 'cat climbing.' You know when you climb, you really stick your gaffs into the pole. (Dad) wouldn't. He just put that gaff on that pole and it wouldn't leave but just a little bitty dent. Everybody remembered him by that because he could climb a pole, and you couldn't hardly tell where he climbed it." David laughs, "And I remember him falling off some poles. One time he fell off a pole three times. He had a tee-shirt on and that third time he didn't have much of a tee-shirt left. We'd call it 'burning a pole.' I think if you burn the pole, you come all the way to the ground. And he would go back up and finish his job."

Tommy Cox recalls, "We went out and was going to work

on the line, and I didn't know what I was getting into. And it was me and Dub Stout and I think Gene Farquhar. Gene had worked here several years. He was a senior lineman. I was at the meter base checking the voltage, but when I turned around, somebody had hollered, and Gene fell off the pole. And that made me wonder if a man had been here a good long period of time . . . If he fell, I know what I'd do. I'd probably fall on my head and get killed. But it was interesting to continue from there on.

"After I seen Gene fall," continues Tommy, "it made me a little spooked of climbing. You'd bury the hooks up. We'd call it 'Stomp the pole,' and you'd make the side of your feet sore if you stomped the pole too hard. That hook would come down and rub your foot. It'd make an indention and bruise your foot. I fell off of several poles."

David says, "Your first instinct is to grab the pole. You don't just automatically stop. You're gonna role your shirt and tee-shirt up under your chin. They tell you to stay away from it, where you won't get splinters all in your belly and your legs, but your instinct is to grab that pole. I tell the young guys, 'If you climb a pole, you're gonna fall. If you go through life without falling or slipping on a pole, you're just going to be fortunate."

Ice Storm of '72

The new generation got their first taste of severe weather when another bad ice storm hit Hill County. Milton Cranfill says, "I'll never forget the ice storm of '72. That's where you find out how bad you want to be a lineman . . . We'd been after it for right about a week ... and the last pole we changed out was down in the ice . . . and it was right on the interstate. And we got that pole changed out. We get on the radio, 'What's next?'" Milton remembers hearing the voice of his dispatcher. "'I believe that's it, everybody. Come on in.' That was probably the best words you could imagine after a whole week of ice. And we were going over the overpass of the interstate and headed home. Ronnie was driving, and I reached over and turned on the radio and a song was coming on. 'Six Days on the Road and I'm Gonna Make It Home Tonight.'

I'll never forget that song because that's what we'd done. We'd been out for six days and finally going home."

Family

"Itasca is a small community," says Larry Farquhar. "And when I started to work for Hill County Electric in 1974, I knew all the employees already and was friends with the majority. As time went by I was not only working with friends, but we became a family. We cared about each other. We helped each other out not only at work, but away from work. My dad worked here when I was a very small child. My brother was working here when I started to work. My brother-in-law worked here. Immediate family aside, we were all family. That's the way we felt, each one of us. We have all been through some good times and tough times, but we made it through together. That's what families do."

Running with the Bull

In 1974, the linemen were working in Grandview, Texas in a pasture filled with cattle when they had a run-in with a bull that didn't like them being on his turf.

William Watson recalls, "My apprentice lineman, Don Wortman, and I were working in Mr. T.J. Harrell's pasture. He had Jersey bulls in this pasture. These spotter bulls are known to have bad attitudes. One of them came over to our work area bellowing and pawing the ground."

David Brackin remembers, "He was a mean one. And our line went across his pasture. We had to get in there with that bull to get our line fixed. And that bull, you had to watch him. He charged the truck."

William says, "Don was working on the pole about eight feet from the ground. The bull started head-butting the rear bumper of our service truck. I guess the bumper was too hard for his head so he moved around the rear quarter panel on the passenger side. It looked like he might turn the truck over from the way he had it bouncing."

David laughs, "We were running around the truck, trying to get away from it, staying on the other side. But he'd paw the ground and just hit the side of the truck."

William says, "I had to get into the truck and drive away to stop the bull. He then bellowed at Don on the pole. Don always said that he couldn't climb higher on the pole without unbuckling his pole strap, but he learned to do so that day. After the bull butted the pole a few times, he went on back to the herd to do his spotting job. And marking had made him a little irritable." William laughs, "We named him 'Cross Fire.'"

The Main Office

While the linemen were having their adventures out in the field, new employees were being hired to work at the Co-op's main office to work as clerks and handle customer service, collections, dispatch, and marketing.

Before coming to Hill County Electric, Bob Wilson worked at an insurance company in Fort Worth, Texas. "I was walking down a dead-end street one night, and two guys ran out of the bushes shooting at each other. And I said, 'Lord, get this butt out of here.' So I quit two days before Christmas in '74. Right after, I went back to my apartment after the first of the year, and Mother called and said she was talking to a lady at church and she happened to be Ralph Bailey's next-door neighbor. She said, 'Ralph is looking for a man to be in the office. Would you think about doing that?' And I said, 'Well, I would, I guess. I don't know.' So I came down and talked to him, and I was a little bit confused when we got through. I didn't know if I was interviewed or what. He didn't ask me to fill out an application or anything. So I got ready to leave and said, 'Thank you for the interview. Do I have the job?' And he said, 'Well yeah, I wouldn't have called you in here if you didn't have the job. You would have never got through this door.' And he said, 'Oh by the way. They're gonna kill me if I don't get an application filled out. Here.' And I asked, 'Do you have a clipboard or something?' And he said, 'You can write on your leg. It's okay.

They don't really need to read it."'

Bob Wilson started out in the customer service department and met with the members face to face. "Back then people walked in every month. You knew their name, you knew their kids." But Bob soon learned that working customer service also meant sometimes dealing with some pretty angry folks. "Back in those days you'd get a customer tell you they were going to come shoot you, something like that."

The staff working collections also heard some creative excuses when a member couldn't pay their bill. William Watson says, "I remember one of the old linemen telling me one time he was trying to collect the bill from an old lady, and she told him that she couldn't pay the bill because her husband done woke up dead."

Bob laughs, "This one lady's mother died six times in three years. They couldn't pay their bill." He'd heard all kinds of stories. His favorite was when a woman told him over the phone, "I'm on insulin. You can't cut me off, because I have to have my icebox for my insulin."

Another challenge to starting a new job at Hill County Electric was learning the linemen's lingo. Bob says, "The linemen all talked slang. I had only been here six months, and everybody kept talking about a pot that was blown. And finally after six months, I said, 'What is a pot?' It's a transformer."

William Watson laughs, "There was a customer called in years ago, and told the lady that answered the phone there was a dead man that had washed up down at his place. And the funny part of it is she asked him if there was a cemetery anywhere around him. Well, the 'dead man' was (slang for) the anchor that holds the line up."

New Leadership

In 1976, the bicentennial year, the leadership of Hill County Electric Cooperative changed once again as Ralph Bailey retired and his second-in-command, G.W. Cates, took over as Manager.

Ralph Bailey shaking hands with G.W. Cates

G.W. Cates (Manager 1976-1984)

When Bob Wilson was growing up in Itasca, he remembers, "G.W. Cates used to hit me over the head with his newspaper every afternoon when he came in. He lived right beside me for many years, and when I was a little kid, we had a picket fence. He'd meet me at the fence every afternoon. He'd hit me over the head with the paper and then he'd give me the paper." Years later Bob ended up working for G.W. at the main office. While Ralph Bailey had been an outgoing manager, highly involved in the community, Bob recalls, "Mr. Cates was a very quiet man. He was not really interested in a lot of community activities. But he was willing to send somebody else to those things, an employee to be a (Hill County Electric) representative."

The Boys in the Field

The linemen were a tight-knit bunch who spent a lot of hours working out in the field together. They climbed poles, installed new lines, repaired lines that were down, and worked through all types of weather. When there was an outage, it didn't matter if it was rain or shine, hot or freezing, the linemen had to be outside working. This created a sense of brotherhood between them.

David Brackin remembers, "A lot of times we'd set outages at night. Ronnie Upchurch, I'd always go on call with him. After we got (the power) on, we'd watch and see if it was going to go back out. If it's out and you have a short on top of a pole, you'll see it blow up or light up. Then you can tell where to go to find the problem. I remember a lot of times working at night, we'd be so tired. We'd go to sleep, and Ronnie would still be watching the line to see if it was going to blink or something. Ronnie would say, 'Did y'all see that?' 'Oh, yeah, we saw that!' We'd never see it blink, because we'd be asleep. Ronnie could go for days without sleep."

Milton Cranfill recalls a time when David Brackin had his own incident. "We were over at the lake, and of course we were young. Ronnie was twenty-six and all of us were twenty-one and twenty-two. David, 'Buck' is what we called him, decided that he was wanting to try some chewing tobacco. And we had driven from the lake down 933 south of Whitney, and we were turning on 1304 and Ronnie lost them in the rearview mirror. And so we went back, and right there at the intersection the digger had run off the road and Buck was down in the ditch throwing up . . . There was always something happening with them two in that truck."

During their lunch breaks or before or after work the linemen often pulled pranks on one another to keep their spirits up. One such prankster was Gary "Shorty" Lewis. The guys called him "Shorty" because he stood five-foot-three. He especially liked to pull pranks on his foreman, Dub Stout. "Dub was deathly scared of snakes," remembers Gary. "We caught a little ole snake and I walked up to Dub, and I said, 'Here.' He said, 'You better get that thing away from me or I'll fire you.' And I said, 'Dub, you can't fire me. You haven't got the authority to do that.' He said, 'I'll kill you then.' We all played jokes on each other."

David Brackin says, "I was deathly scared of stinging scorpions. They'd cut the tail off and come after me. I hated those things. They could run me to death with a stinging scorpion."

Larry Farquhar recalls, "One time Gary Lewis wanted to hide from our crew foreman, Dub Stout, and make him think we left him at the warehouse. Gary wanted my brother, Gene, and myself to shut him up in the big tool box on the side of the digger truck and tell Dub that we forgot him when we got to the first job. This tool box is where we kept climbing tools, teeth for the rock bits, hand tools, etc."

"I got in there," says Gary. "It was a pretty good size tool-box. I should have taken everything out of there. But it was several miles to the next job and I rode in that thing down a gravel road and they were beating me to death."

Larry laughs, "We stopped at the country store every morning to get a snack and a soda. When we got to the store, Gary was beating on the door of the toolbox and yelling to let him out. When we opened the door, he crawled out covered in dust, coughing, choking, spitting, and yelling about how the tools were about to beat him to death. Dub wished we had left him."

Two of the biggest pranksters were the Upchurch brothers, especially to each other. Larry recalls, "Ronnie had a blue denim cowboy hat that he wore every day, summer and winter. As time passed, that hat had collected dirt and dust and Ronnie's sweat and really began to look rather bad. Kenneth told Ronnie that he was going to tell their mom to have him throw that hat away if he didn't. Well, Ronnie didn't want to get rid of his hat. One day while Kenneth was digging a hole for a pole, he finished digging and got off the digger and went to Ronnie's truck while Ronnie was helping to frame the pole, and got Ronnie's beloved blue denim cowboy hat and threw it into the hole. He never told Ronnie until after we had set the pole on top of it and shoveled in the dirt and tamped it in around the pole. Seemed pretty funny to us at the time."

Ice Storm of '78

At the latter half of the decade another terrible winter storm hit Central Texas. The heavy ice weighing down the power lines caused a lot of outages. David Brackin remembers, "We worked non-stop for two or three days, and then went home, got a little sleep, and then came back. It got us good. That was probably one of the worst ones I'd been through, with all the cold and everything being down."

Ronnie remembers how the ice storm outages affected their manager. "G.W. worried constantly. You'd walk in the morning and he looked like he didn't have a friend left. We'd tell him, 'It's gonna be all right. It's gonna be fine. We're gonna get it on one of these days.' He'd say, 'Yeah, I know, but y'all are sure working hard.' He was as concerned for us as well as our members."

"The weather didn't clear up," says Kenneth. "And they decided it was going to be longer than we first thought and longer than the weather people thought. We'd come to work at seven in the morning and worked till it got good and dark. "

Ronnie says, "And when we'd quit, we would go to the café and get something to eat, and the company would pay for it, and then we'd come home. And be up there the next morning. Every line we got on we climbed the poles. They had contractors in here, and they all had buckets. We just carried our digger and carried some poles on it. And if we had to climb a pole and it looked like something was going to happen to it like that we'd just back in there, dig a hole and set us a new pole."

"You could just barely get around," says Kenneth. "We had one four-wheel drive pick-up at that time, and Rock had it. Milton and I rode together and Rock and his brother-in-law (Larry Farquhar) rode together, and part of the time if we were going up a hill, he was pushing us up the hill. We were working a lot down (at this one section around Abbott). And there was one fellow down there. Every time he'd come by it seemed like one of our trucks was stuck, and he had a four-wheel drive."

"It was our mechanic's dad who helped," remembers Milton Cranfill. "Every time we come down the road we were stuck somewhere. We didn't have chains. We just crawled along the road to keep moving on that ice."

Kenneth says, "And if he'd come by, and we were away from Rock, he'd pull us back up on the road. There's tremendous people out here."

During those icy storms the linemen were aided by many good-natured people—members of the Co-op—who wanted to make their job a little more bearable. Ronnie says, "I was standing out in this guy's front yard with a long stick hitting at limbs, knocking the ice off of them and getting them up off the line. And this old man walked up to me and just started feeling (my coat) and said, 'Where's your pocket?' And I told him, 'What do you want to know where my pocket is for?' And he said, 'I'm gonna give you this bottle of whiskey.' He just stuck that bottle in my pocket. And I told him, 'I can't drink that. I'm working.' And he said, 'My gosh, son, you're gonna quit some time, aren't you?' That's always stood out for me."

Kenneth had his own encounter with a kind member. "This guy lived on the very end of a line and it was going up through a whole bunch of trees. And we got over there one afternoon, about four o'clock, I guess, and it was just trees, trees, trees up through there. Well we started to work on it. Right after dark his wife made a pot of coffee and sent that coffee up there to us. I've told him and her since then, that was the best coffee I've ever had in my life."

After the ice storm and seeing how often the linemen's trucks got stuck in the mud, G.W. Cates bought two brand new four-wheel-drive trucks. After that it became standard for linemen to work with four-wheel-drive vehicles.

By the end of the 1970s, Jimmy Carter was President. The Cold War with the Communist Soviet Union was still very much in effect. After the NASA Space Program cancelled several space missions, due to nearly losing the astronauts of Apollo 13 in 1975, NASA focused on developing the space shuttle. Popular movies were *Alien*, *Apocalypse Now*, and *Kramer vs. Kramer*. Disco was fading out as America got ready to turn another corner into a new decade. In Itasca, Hill County Electric was still growing strong and headed into the Eighties with great momentum.

"I hope the people on Wall Street will pay attention to the people on Main Street. If they do, they will see there is a rising tide of confidence in the future of America."

— President Ronald Reagan
September 1981

CHAPTER EIGHT

The 1980s:
The Reagan Era

The 1980s in the U.S. kicked off with a change in leadership, as Republican candidate Ronald Reagan was elected to become the 40th President in 1980. With a strong economy, it was a booming time for business and technology. Steven Jobs, co-founder of Apple, Inc., revolutionized home computers with the introduction of the mouse-based MacIntosh. IBM came up with their own version of the personal computer. Meanwhile, Bill Gates of Microsoft created Windows, making it easier for users to interface with computers. NASA was once again a success with the launch of the Columbia Space Shuttle in 1981. The children of the Hippy Generation became the "Me Generation" as yuppies and preppies, wearing Izod and Polo shirts and designer jeans, focused on self-gratification and racked up massive debts on credit cards. Popular movies were *Back to the Future*, *Indiana Jones*, and *E.T. The Extra Terrestrial*.

For Hill County Electric Cooperative, the '80s was a period of steady economic growth, as Manager G.W. Cates ran the operation as smoothly as his predecessors. With the Co-op growing in member size, the linemen continued to build new power lines across five counties.

Pole Stories

"Every lineman has a pole that he remembers very distinctly," says Kenneth Upchurch. "I remember one morning we had a line down. The poles were old poles to start with. But this was a single-phase pole that had two wires on it. Both wires were down. So we decided if we could get up there and get two on it, and bring both wires up together, then it would be less strain on the other poles down the line than it would if we just got up there and pulled one wire up. So another guy, 'Coonie' (Allen Howe), and I climbed this pole, and he was above me. We got the wire up and we were working it up together. And I don't know what happened, but both of those wires broke at the same time. Coonie's hoist and everything that he had up above me was falling on me. For just a second, I could not figure out what happened. And I looked up and he was trying to get his strap off to jump into a tree, because it was just going like that. For just a second, I couldn't figure out what was going on."

Ronnie Upchurch recalls, "I climbed poles for right at forty years. I never got scared but on one pole. Right out here at Ross Road, I got on top of a pole one morning. It was right about fifty yards off the interstate, and Milton was on the ground. And trucks were running up and down that dad gum interstate, and I told Milton, 'Boy if one of those trucks lost control and hit this pole, I'd been in a mess, wouldn't I?' And I had no more got that out of my mouth, till there's a guy coming down that interstate that was hauling trailer house frames. And (one) frame was sticking up. And when he went under the overpass, that dad gum trailer house frame slapped the bottom of the overpass, and for just the minute that scared the devil out of me."

Lineman belted to a pole

121

Milton Cranfill remembers a particular pole. "Me and Ronnie were changing out a four-way junction pole, and just set the new pole and now we're up working on it. And it was a little bit of rise, a hill. I'm on one side of the pole and I'm looking north and Ronnie is facing south, moving wire ... and just out of the blue, coming down the fence line out in the field a plane had come by, and he was going to crop dust this field. And I'm looking over Ronnie's shoulder and all of a sudden here's a plane that's a hundred yards out and six feet off the ground and we're forty foot in the air. And the pilot came straight for our poles, and naturally as he got ten feet from us he went straight over our heads. We could've slapped the tires on it. We paused for a minute and then went on back to work."

Larry Farquhar says, "There was a time when we were wrecking out the lines in an area that a new lake was going to flood. We were pulling some of the old poles with the digger truck. Kenneth Upchurch was operating the digger. We were pulling an old stump of a pole that had been sawn off about four foot above ground level. Kenneth put pressure on the pole and it would not come out of the ground, so he revved the engine on the digger up and applied more pressure. All of the sudden the pole broke just under the top of the ground and the stump (about five or six foot long) flew up in the air about fifteen-twenty feet above Kenneth. The winch cable was still attached and the pole was flipping end over end. Those of us on the ground ran to get away from the stump, but Kenneth did not have time to get off the digging machine. The pole came back down and missed Kenneth, but it sure gave us all quite a scare."

A Monumental Improvement: Bucket Trucks

One of the most positive impacts on the safety of the linemen occurred in 1983, when the first bucket trucks were introduced. No longer did they have to scale poles with belts and spiked boots. And the risk of electrocution was reduced to nearly zero. William Watson says, "With the insulated bucket trucks we don't have to turn power off. We used to use hot sticks, and worked off the pole. Of course, our safety rules forbid us to touch a hot power line, even though we have rubber gloves on. But now with the bucket trucks, you still use rubber gloves, rubber sleeves, cover-up materials, that you can work hot lines. And it's safe if you follow the rules."

Lineman working with rubber gloves and a hot stick

A New Sheriff in Town

Sam Houston (Manager 1984 - 1995)

In the spring of 1984, G.W. Cates retired and Sam Houston was hired as Manager. For the first time in nearly fifty years, the board of directors hired a manager who had not worked for the Co-op before. But Sam Houston immediately carried on the tradition of treating his employees like family. Wesley Brackin remembers working under Sam, "He was real nice because he was a preacher. An Evangelist from Woodrow, in a church west of here . . . If you needed something, tools or tire or something, all you had to do was ask him and he'd say, 'I'll look into it.' And usually he got it for you. He was that type of guy."

"I love Sam," says Milton Cranfill. "Super guy, super boss. If you didn't like working for Sam, there was something wrong with you . . . Back in the day when I started, our starting time was eight o'clock (in the morning). And people like me and Tommy, Gary Lewis, somewhere between six-thirty and seven we were here in the linemen's room at least an hour every day ahead of time . . . Well, Sam and I would usually be in that break room six, six-thirty every morning drinking coffee."

Kenneth Upchurch says, "Sam would get here every morning about six o'clock. Rock and I and Rock's brother-in-law, (Larry Farquhar), and our brother-in-law, Milton Cranfill—we would get here about six-fifteen or six-thirty and sit in there with Sam every morning. It was hilarious. People would just come into work and that's where they'd congregate. The break room. Sam would get here and make the coffee."

Sam was not only friendly to the staff, he had an immediate impact on everyone's wages. "When he got here," says Ronnie Upchurch, "he contacted the guy from the REA in Washington, and that man came down and reviewed all our salaries. And he was going to see how our salaries worked compared to everybody else's. I came to work one morning and I was making $4.25 an hour. When I went home that afternoon I was making over $12 an hour." Sam Houston took pride in taking care of his employees. Ronnie says, "He told us, 'I've done several of these, and everyone I've ever done, everybody is making more when I leave. They're not making less.'"

Kenneth remembers another time, "They had a county show down here every year and all the schools in the county had their livestock show. Sam encouraged you to go down there. He said, 'Park that truck.' I said, 'Well, I'll come get my truck.' Sam said, 'No, no, no. Park that company truck down there. Let people see it down there.' He would encourage you to do stuff like that."

Manager Sam Houston speaking at an annual member meeting

A band plays for the members at the meeting

A member wins a $100 gift certificate

The Computer Age

Hill County Electric Co-op's first computers

In the mid '80s, desktop computers were starting to be implemented into the work forces of companies across the nation. When Debbie Cole came on board in October of 1984, she had recently left a large investor-owned utility company that had a very advanced computer system. She was expecting Hill County Electric to be current with technology. "When I interviewed I didn't pay a lot of attention to the office furnishings. I was just excited to not have to commute back to Ft. Worth anymore. I came in and sat down and got my stuff in my desk and got ready to work and after about an hour I went to the lady next to me and said, 'Where are our computers?' She got a big chuckle out of that because they were still doing everything with paper. As far as all their orders, they wrote their payments down on paper and then we would send it to Brazos Electric, and they would actually post the payments. So it was about a two-day gap in between. We would ship it there and two days later they would ship it back and actually show who had paid."

To keep up with the changing times, in 1985 Sam purchased desktop computers for the staff at the main office. Not everyone was ready for the change, however, so Sam used a subtle tactic.

William Watson

William Watson, a former lineman who was now working in the office, remembers Sam "knew how to ease you in to using the computer. He told me he was going to set one on my desk, and said, 'You don't have to use it.' Of course, I had to keep up with my other work, too, and had to learn this computer."

Bob Wilson, who had taken a job in member services, remembers getting a new computer. "Sam said, 'You don't have to worry. You'll never have to use the computer, but we're going to have them. And the secretarial staff will be using them if you need anything typed.' That was the time the company started realizing that they needed to do more training on Excel and Word." Eventually Bob, William, and everyone on staff had to adapt and learn how to work with a computer.

Major Milestone

In 1985, Hill County Electric Cooperative celebrated their 50th Anniversary.

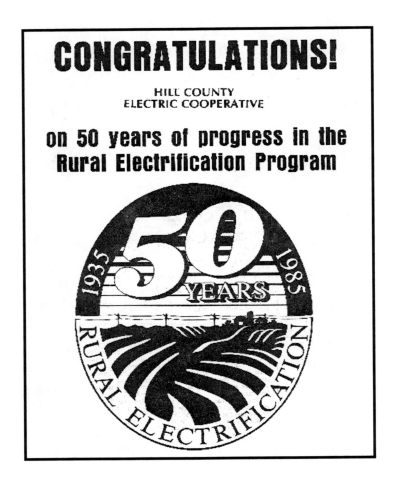

**Sam Houston presenting a gift book
to Pauline Farrow**

The Women at the Office

Back in the '80s, the Co-op's board of directors and managerial staff were made up entirely of men, and women employees were treated differently than they are today. Debbie Cole recalls what it was like when she first started working here. "We actually had a policy that when the linemen came into the office, that the ladies would treat them as if they were a member. That was the courtesy that we were supposed to show the linemen when they came to turn in paperwork."

From Left: Bob Wilson, Debbie Cole, Rhonda Trejo,
Sam Houston and Carolyn Bons

Rhonda Trejo joined the office staff in February 1986. She worked with Debbie Cole and Carolyn Bons in the customer service department as an assistant cashier. "The three of us were tied to a pole," says Rhonda.

Debbie laughs, "When they designed the building there were only plugs in the middle column in the office. So none of us could get farther than three feet from that pole. We were cramped into a ten-by-ten-foot area where all of our desks met."

At the time, Rhonda had never worked on a computer before. "The computer hated me the first week. It didn't want to let me in." But Rhonda did get along well with people. "I liked working with the members. Took payments. Handled phone calls. And dispatched on nights and weekends."

During storms when there were a lot of outages, Debbie, Carolyn, and Rhonda helped dispatch. Debbie recalls, "If we knew we needed to come, we showed up at all hours of the night to help the linemen answer the phone so they could start dispatching on the radio. You never knew what we were going to look like when we showed up. We knew we were really going to catch it from the guys, because we showed up looking really good a lot of times at two and three in the morning. One of us always managed to grab food coming out of the house, because you really didn't know when you were going to get to eat."

Some nights they worked dispatch, but not very many calls came in, so they found themselves working the graveyard shift with not a lot to do. Debbie says, "We didn't have internet, so we had to entertain ourselves. One of the favorite pastimes was to have chair races in the office chairs. We would do that down the hall."

Ronnie Upchurch remembers some of the fun times spent at the main office during stormy weather. "We had a linemen's room with a pool table in it and when it was rainy bad weather, rather than go out and ride around, everybody stayed in. And they'd play dominoes, and (Sam Houston) would come down and play dominoes with us and shoot pool and just sit and talk and visit."

Showdown

For a time, linemen were responsible for collecting checks for unpaid utility bills. If the member wasn't willing to pay his bill, the linemen were instructed to kill the power to the house. This sometimes led to some dangerous situations with irate home-owners.

Kenneth Upchurch and Tommy Cox remember a time when they were working together and got assigned to collect a check. They drove up to Midlothian one night to set a meter back. The long driveway wound around the house. The man came out of his back door holding something behind his back.

Tommy said to Kenneth, "Did you see what he has?"

Kenneth nodded. "He's got a gun." This worried him, because there was no way he could back out the truck fast enough. He told Tommy, "T.C., I'll let you set the meter and I'll watch this guy."

They stepped out and Kenneth grabbed the new meter from the toolbox. As they approached with the bill stating the amount of money he owed, the man hid the pistol behind his back. Tommy did the talking. Kenneth eased up as close to the man as he could get. He remembers, "I had the meter in my hand. And he had the gun straight down beside his leg. I told myself, if he brings that pistol up, if it clears his leg, he's getting this meter in the side of the head."

Tommy laughs about his partner, "He was going to cold-cock him if he tried to pull that gun and shoot either one of us, because Kenneth's a pretty good size ole boy. And I was little with a big mouth." They set the meter back and explained that they were only here to collect a check, keeping their watchful eyes on the man's gun.

Kenneth says, "He talked to us a little while and went in the house to get the money, and when he came back, he didn't have his pistol."

Encounters with Animals

The territory that Hill County Electric Cooperative serviced covered hundreds of square miles of Central Texas. They worked on desolate highways, farms, ranch land, and wooded areas around lakes and creeks. Working in the field gave the linemen plenty of opportunities to come across all kinds of wild animals.

Larry Farquhar says, "In our line of work here in Texas, you always will have encounters with snakes. Birds tend to build nests on the transformers and other equipment on the lines and the snakes will slither up the poles or wires and sometimes end up getting fried in the process. One time we were moving a line near Whitney for a road widening. David Brackin was running one of the digging machines. He was digging the hole where we were moving the pole off the roadway about ten feet or so. When he ran the bit down one time and brought it out of ground to sling dirt off the bit, there was a rattlesnake that he had pulled up out of the hole mixed in the dirt. When he slung the dirt off the bit, the snake was more than a little irritated."

Larry remembers another snake story. "We were eating lunch one summer day under a couple of trees. Someone saw something moving through the tall grass several yards away. As we checked it out, you could see rattles above the grass. Everyone got up and picked some rocks up. Gary Lewis picked up a tree limb that was about four or five feet long."

Gary laughs, "I had a stick that wasn't near long enough to kill him. He was a big ole rattlesnake. At least five or six-feet long. Had about nine or ten rattles."

Larry says, "Gary looked at his tree limb, looked at the snake, and then tossed the tree limb and ran to the digging machine. He got the wooden tamp from the digger. The tamp was eight feet long. He then ran back to the snake and killed it."

Gary smiles. "I skinned him and tanned his hide."

Milton Cranfill remembers another snake story. "One time, during the summer, as we were changing out poles, we got the wire off this pole and pulling it out of the ground. Now the pole starts coming out of the ground—it sets six-foot deep—when it's three or four foot out of the ground, you'll instinctively walk over and put your hand up under it, guide it to the digger. And somewhere in that last foot when the bottom of the pole comes out of the ground about four snakes come with it. And we're all standing there about a foot from this hole and now there are four little rattlesnakes at our feet. It puts you backing up, I tell you that."

Snakes weren't the only animals the linemen encountered. "We saw a lot of coyotes," says Dub Stout. "One morning we was going down south of Hillsboro, and one ran across the road in front of us, and about a couple hundred yards out there was a barbed wire fence. That coyote tried to leap over that fence, when he went right over the top wire and tripped over and he had that wire crossways over his coat over the fence. Boy you talk about having a fit. But he finally got loose."

The linemen also had to work around animals at ranches. Often times, the linemen got called into to fix a pole that had fallen to the ground. Kenneth says, "It has a neutral bracket and if it hits the ground, sometimes that neutral bracket holds the hot wire off the ground. Well, they called in here one time about a pole down, so we got down there."

The Upchurch brothers drove out to a ranch to answer the call. Ronnie says, "They had a pole fell and it was hot, and I can't remember how many dad gum cows got killed. It seemed like it was ten to twelve."

Kenneth says, "We thought the line was dead. But we checked and it was still hot." It was several inches from the ground. "We killed the line out and grounded it and everything. And when we got out there to where it was, there was a dead cow and a dead calf and a jack rabbit, all side by side, laying there. The jack rabbit, about two inches down on his ears had been burned off."

Tommy Cox recalls a time he rescued a dog. "We was out building a line and changing a transformer, and I heard a dog bark. And I told them boys, 'I think a dog's barking, but it's a muffled sound.' Nobody paid any attention, but I'm an animal lover. I went over to check the voltage on the house and when I did, I heard the muffled sound again. I went around the house and notice a little door on the edge of the house, that I could get under the house. And I thought, this here is rattlesnake country. So I put a flashlight in there and at the other end of the house is a little pup that had his head stuck."

"And I crawled under the house. Took a chance on getting bit by a rattler. That dog was stuck and couldn't get out. So I set my flashlight up and took me some pliers. I was afraid he was gonna bite me, so I had on gloves. I broke (the wall) out enough with the pliers that he could get out. He shot out of there and that was the last time I had seen that dog. I saved his life. He would have been a dead little dog."

Kids of the Linemen

Kenneth Upchurch's boys (Coy & Kerry)

Hill County Electric was a family-oriented business and many of the staff's children have grown up to work for the Co-op. Their love of the company began early on when the kids went on service jobs with their fathers and watched them work on the poles. "Back then they went to work with us," says Kenneth. "And Milton, our brother-in-law, and our nephew, Greg, would come. The three kids would ride in the digger with us. They saw what we do. They saw how much fun we had . . . They had a blast."

"I remember Dad being on-call," says Crystal Upchurch, Ronnie's daughter. "I remember the phone ringing, him answering the phone and then going off to work. I remember him looking at maps. He taught me how to read the grids. And so when he'd get a call he'd say, 'If anyone needs to find me, I'll be at so-and-so grid.'" Crystal also got the chance to go out into the field with her father. "Dad would get calls, and he'd always ask me, 'Do you want to go with me?' And I'd hop in the truck with him and go on out to the outages." She would sit in the truck and watch her father work. "When he would be on call, he'd take a bucket truck home with him, and I thought that was just the bee's knees. And I would crawl into the bucket and he'd let me go up and down and up and down right there in our front yard."

Farewell to Dub

In 1986, Dub Stout retired after thirty-nine years of service. Dub had started working as a truck driver and pole digger back in 1947. He later worked as a lineman and crew foreman and eventually moved into a leadership position at the office. He retired as Staff Engineer. Hill County Electric threw him a party to remember in the Farrow Room.

**Dub Stout putting on his new Stetson
while wife, Margaret, and two co-workers look on**

Hidden Relic

The Texas range land in which the linemen work had been roamed by Indians during the previous centuries. Scattered among the rocks and cactus one can find flint arrowheads, crude knife blades, rocks marked with symbols, and other artifacts. Tommy Cox recalls an interesting tale about a relic he discovered back in 1988. "We was going toward Blum and I needed to stop and go to the rest room. And we don't have no rest rooms, no potties on the back of the truck. So we stopped and I go under a bridge, and I'm doing my business and I looked up on the ledge of the bridge and there's a skull under the railing of the bridge. And I thought, where did that skull come from? So I climbed up in there, and some jaw teeth was up there with the skull. So we got on the radio and called the police, and they come out there. And they was taking pictures and everything. It was an Indian skull. The police told me that it had washed up there. What I figured is somebody robbed an Indian grave and got scared and hid (the skull) and was gonna come back to get it. The sheriff's department took it to Hillsboro and put it in the museum. They had it analyzed and said it was dated back to 1855."

The Eighties came to a close on a high note. In 1987, President Reagan and Soviet General Secretary Gorbachev signed the INF Treaty, bringing about the end of the Cold War. Two years later, in 1989, the Fall of the Berlin Wall symbolized the collapse of Communism and was one of the most momentous events of the decade. After serving two terms from 1981-1989, President Reagan retired and George H.W. Bush became the 41st President of the United States. In Itasca, Sam Houston had become part of the Hill County Electric family and the staff were happy to work for the Co-op.

"When I took office, only high energy physicists had ever heard of what is called the World Wide Web ... Now even my cat has its own page."

— President Bill Clinton
1996 announcement of
The Next Generation Internet Initiative

"Life is like a box of chocolates. You never know what your gonna get."

— Forrest Gump

CHAPTER NINE

The 1990s:
Growing in Leaps and Bounds

The 1990s signified a time of economical and technological advancement. The World Wide Web went public, connecting people around the globe like never before. Internet businesses quickly followed and e-commerce offered alternative ways to shop. Communicating through email and cell phones became the norm. In music, Seattle bands like Nirvana spawned the Grunge movement, a subgenre of Alternative Rock. Hip-hop music also became mainstream. Country western music took on a new sound with the emergence of singers like Garth Brooks, Clint Black, Brooks & Dunn, and Faith Hill.

In space exploration, NASA sent the Hubble Space Telescope up into orbit to observe stars and planets from a closer perspective. Around the world democracy spread and communism lost momentum as the U.S.S.R. dissolved its union of Soviet republics. Iraq, under the dictatorship of Saddam Hussein, invaded Kuwait which led to the Gulf War. President George H. W. Bush served one term until January, 1993, when President

Bill Clinton took over. Women were assuming more and more leadership roles in business and politics. In Texas, Anne Richards was the second female Governor until 1994 when she was defeated for re-election by future president, George W. Bush.

The Nineties was also a decade of growth for Hill County Electric. By the end of 1990, the Co-op had 11,883 active members and would continue to grow year after year.

Debbie Cole recalls, "We started our growth in the '90s. There are so many co-ops across the nation that are just stale. They are seeing no growth whatsoever. That's not true for our Co-op. Our northern area has really been our area that has grown. That's because a lot of people are moving out of Dallas area and into more suburban places."

The development of multiple subdivisions in North Texas led to a competition between Hill County and Ellis County to see who could be the more prominent county.

Debbie says, "Hill County has always been the dominant area with the most members in it. Then in the '90s, when the growth started in Ellis County, there's been a competition that Ellis County was going to take over Hill County. That's been an ongoing thing for several years now."

Farewell to Wesley Brackin

On March 1, 1990, Hill County Electric said farewell to another long-standing employee as former lineman, Wesley Brackin, retired after forty-four years of service. Hill County Electric threw him a retirement party in the Farrow Room.

Wesley Brackin with Mrs. Farrow and retired Executive Secretary Trudy Cole (far left)

Wesley with wife, Rosie, and Sam Houston

The Superconducting Super Collider

In 1991, construction of a particle acceleration complex began on the outskirts of Waxahachie, Texas. The Super Collider was a giant underground ring, shaped like an oval, with two ring pipes that circled 54 miles and surrounded Waxahachie. The purpose of the lab and underground tunnels was for physicists to study the reaction to colliding protons. While the building of the Superconducting Super Collider promised an advancement in energy, it had a negative effect on some of Hill County Electric's members.

Debbie Cole says, "One of my saddest memories of working in the office was when the Super Collider was going to be built in our northern area. The land of many long-time residences was consumed by the program and they had to move. I can remember people calling and crying when they had their service disconnected, because many of them were having to move off farms that had been in their families for fifty to seventy-five years. It was very sad."

The Super Collider project received harsh criticism for its extremely high budgets and its competition for government funds with the NASA program. Even though President Bill Clinton pushed to move forward with the building of the Super Collider, Congress cancelled the project in 1993.

The Angry Wives Club

One of the issues that Sam Houston had to reconcile was the situation with the Co-op's members calling the linemen's personal telephone lines during outages. While the linemen tolerated sharing their phone line for company business, the wives were growing tired of it.

Ronnie Upchurch's daughter, Crystal, says, "I remember Mom talking about a meeting they all had when the wives were fed up, and they were like 'Hey, we're not doing this anymore. We have to work.' My mom was vice president of a bank here in Itasca. She had to get up the next morning and go to work . . . I remember my mom telling me they were in this meeting, and there was a comment made, 'Well, your husband gets paid to be on call.' My aunt was like, 'Yeah, and they earn every damn penny of it.' And they didn't compensate (the wives) in any way and it probably hurt them. They had to get up the next morning."

The frustrated wives of the linemen rallied together, refusing to answer phones. Ronnie Upchurch recalls, "Sam was the one who made the change when he got the diverter."

Kenneth Upchurch says, "It was just a device that if they called in it would divert it from that number to your number at your house."

Bob Wilson, who worked at the main office, remembers, "We had a button here at the counter and we switched it, and that line was transferred from here over to that lineman's house. That was pretty crude technology. It was almost like a walkie-talkie, but they answered it at their house."

Ronnie says, "If you were on call, you turned that switch on. If you were off, and you weren't answering it, you'd just turn it off."

Kenneth says, "That was good in a way, but in a way it was bad, because it took away your private phone, because they used the same line. So there'd be times that my family was on the phone, if they get a call, well they're gonna get a busy signal. That's all it amounted to but yet your family was hampered a little bit, because you didn't have complete freedom with your phone. You felt like you needed to get on and get off."

The diverter provided a temporary solution until the Co-op finally set up a twenty-four-hour dispatching department in-house a few years later, in 1998. This relieved the linemen of ever having to answer telephones at their homes again. "I don't know who was happier," says Debbie Cole, "the linemen or their wives."

Strange Tales from Lineman Tommy Cox

Milton Cranfill remembers what it was like to work out in the field with Tommy Cox. "Tommy was a master comedian. If he can stir something up, it's going to get done." Fondly called "T.C." by his buddies, Tommy had a knack for attracting strange occurrences and awkward situations.

Knocking at Death's Door

One time, Tommy Cox and his partner, Kris Watson, drove out to the lake to fix a line for a house. While working, they noticed a couple of women beating on the front door. Wondering what the fuss was about, Tommy approached them and asked if they needed help with anything.

The women looked distraught. One of them said, "We

haven't seen our friend in a while, and we were wondering if she was in the house."

Tommy tried the front door but it was locked. He went around the back of the house, trying to see if he could get in through a back door. It was also locked. Kris went around the opposite side, opened a window, and crawled into the house. He let Tommy in. The women stayed outside. The house was quiet and musty with a foul odor. Tommy and Kris went into the back living room, and the woman they were looking for was slumped in a chair, dead.

"She was an elderly lady," remembers Tommy. "She had been dead probably for a day. I told Kris, 'Well, we need to check to see if there's anybody else in here.' We didn't know, it could have been a murder."

So Tommy checked the back part of the house, but thankfully there was no killer hiding back there. "When I come back, Kris had his back turned to me and I reached over and grabbed him and he jumps, 'Don't do that!'"

After getting spooked, they went back outside and told the women what they had found. Tommy and Kris called 911 and the Justice of the Peace, and they came over and pronounced the woman dead.

High Voltage

Tommy recalls one crazy incident when he tried to help out a woman who was having trouble with her voltage. "We was trying to figure out the problem and never could figure it out. We had a generator at the office, so we took that generator over. She said her TV wasn't working, that it didn't have enough power. I said, 'Let's crank that generator up and see if we can get her TV to work.' We pulled our pickup up next to the house and had that generator in the back of the pickup. And we run the extension cord through the window and hooked up to the TV. We cranked the generator up, and we never checked the voltage. And that generator was putting out about a hundred and thirty volts. A lot more than what that TV could stand. And we, or I, burnt that TV set up. I felt bad about doing it. I managed to get the money to buy the woman another TV."

The Members Who Wore No Clothes

For a time, Hill County Electric provide electrical service to a nudist resort. Each campsite had poles with a place for trailers and RVs to plug into. Tommy somehow got assigned this area and usually drove out there either to set a meter or disconnect one. "We had a disconnect, and the only thing I ever seen was a nasty old man. He was naked up there, running around with some women. But the women were clothed." Fortunately by the time Tommy got up there to check the meter the man had the decency to put on some clothes.

Another time Tommy was reading meters up toward Midlothian near a lake. "I was looking for a meter, and I walked up on a woman who was sunbathing and didn't have on any clothes. She wasn't even wearing a pair of socks. It scared me, because I didn't want that woman to think that I was a Peeping Tom. I didn't want to get fired, so I called on the radio. I told (the dispatcher), 'I just wanted y'all to know, I'm calling in because I walked up on a lady that didn't have any clothes on.' Of course, she covered herself up with a blanket. We've drove up on several people sunbathing."

A Celebrity Sighting

Tommy Cox recalls the time he came upon a famous actor. "I was over at the lake going to check out a meter and he was walking down the road. I glanced up and looked at him and said, 'No, it can't be.' I looked at him and said, 'Sir, has anybody told you that you look like Chester on *Gunsmoke*?' He said, 'I am Chester on *Gunsmoke*.'" The actor was Dennis Weaver, also well known for starring in the TV show *McCloud* and movies like *Duel* and *Touch of Evil*.

Tommy laughs, "There wasn't nobody there but me and him and a dog. I told him, 'Sir, I'd love to have a picture. I've got a camera, but it's just me and you and that dog.' Well, that dog can't take no picture. I said, 'If you would, would you stand over by my truck so I can tell people that I seen a movie star and that I have proof?' And he said, 'I sure would.'"

Actor Dennis Weaver posing in front of Tommy's truck

New Leadership, New Direction

General Manager Jody Forman (1995-1998)

In 1995, Sam Houston retired and an interim manager served for a few months. Then Jody Forman was hired as General Manager. Jody had come from another company.

Milton Cranfill recalls, "The co-ops were in a transition period. Up through Sam's era, the managers were (typically) co-op employees. It got to the point that you needed someone to run the operation side—the maintenance, the service, the construction—but then also you had to have that business man, too, to keep you in line with finances. Jody was that guy. He came in and turned Hill County Electric from a co-op into a business. You had to have that kind of financial understanding."

While Jody only managed the Co-op for three years, he had an impact and made some permanent changes to Hill

County Electric, starting with the annual member meetings.

Bob Wilson says, "The year that Jody was taking over, was the first year that we actually fed everybody, actually gave (the Members) a free meal. Now before that, when I first came to work here, people would bring sandwiches and blankets and stay on the football field. They'd dance on the track. And then we let service clubs do it one time, and the Rotary Club made hamburgers and we sold them to the members."

The year that Jody came on board was the first year they didn't have the annual members meeting on the football field. "We had it at the County Extension Barn," remembers Bob, "and we had no air conditioning or anything. And in July, we liked to die. Jody talked to me and said, 'We've got to do something about this meeting.' So the board decided they wanted to do a picnic. And how that came about is because they really wanted to try to increase the attendance. The first year we just had a picnic at West, and then we wanted to try and get the northern people more involved, so we started to have the picnic in Waxahachie. They're totally different for the fact that we have a country band up north, and they like a Czech band down south. So that's the reason we got started with picnics."

Another major change under Jody Forman's reign was renaming the company in 1997 from Hill County Electric Cooperative to HILCO.

Main Office in Itasca with new sign

Debbie Cole says, "It was felt the name change was needed because people thought we just served Hill County, when we actually serve five counties: Hill, Ellis, Johnson, McLennan, and Dallas." Those five counties are divided up into seven districts. Each district is headed by a director who is part of HILCO's board.

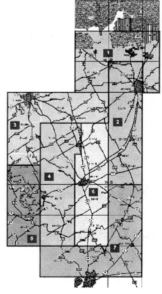

HILCO's Board of Directors

Back Row: Swede Larson, Harvey Kelley, Byron Smith,
Martha McGregor, K.W. McPherson, Steve Sawyer and Jody Forman

Front Row: Moe Craddock, Margaret Hill, Harry Frank Holland
and Gene Heitmiller

The Board Members are elected by the districts to represent the
other Members of the Cooperative and to set policies, bylaws,
and tariffs for the Cooperative to function. The Board hires the
General Manager and instructs the GM on the goals of the Cooperative. The Board reviews and approves the annual budget
as presented by the staff and monitors that budget throughout
the year. The Board also plays a vital part in the political circle
for cooperatives. Board Members devote a lot of time to state

and national legislation, meeting with elected officials in an effort to insure cooperatives are always treated in a fair manner in an effort to keep electric service dependable and affordable to HILCO's Members.

Board members gathered at a meeting at HILCO's main office

For decades, co-ops were predominately run by men. It wasn't until after the '80s that women started getting power in the workforce of the utility companies. In 1995, Margaret Hill was elected as the first female board member, representing District 2, Ellis County. She has held that position for over fifteen years.

Margaret Hill

Harry Frank Holland

Another notable board member, Harry Frank Holland, had first been elected in June 1960. "We all called him 'Harry Frank,'" remembers Debbie. "Nobody used his last name. He was from the Abbott area, which was HILCO's CCN. At one time I know Harry Frank was the mayor and maybe the J.P. and held several offices in Abbott all at once. He was a very prominent figure in the Abbott area. He was very knowledgeable of the co-op operations. What I have always said about Harry Frank is that he was one of the few people in his generation that you saw was quick to adapt and advance with the times. If it was better and safer and more efficient, he was always doing it, where as a lot of people from that generation weren't. Harry Frank was always pushing for better and more efficient ways, especially when it came to the linemen. As far as equipment and stuff like that, he would push for it."

Harry Frank Holland with country western legend Willie Nelson

One year Willie Nelson was the entertainer for the National NRECA convention. Debbie says, "Harry Frank was good friends with Willie's family, because they were from Abbott. He took all of our board members and general managers on Willie's bus to meet Willie, and gave him a HILCO hat and told him he expected him to have that on stage when he performed that night and Willie did. He was on stage with the HILCO cap on."

Expanding Services & Technology

In 1997, the long-time Mom and Pop water supply companies were closing and no one was there to manage these companies. HILCO responded by providing management service for several water supply companies to insure the Co-op members kept quality service.

In 1998, HILCO's first District Office was opened in Whitney, Texas.

First district office in Whitney

As computer technology advanced, meter readers turned in their pencils and paper for hand-held meter reading computers.

**Lee Roy Gonzales reading a meter
with a hand-held computer**

Farewell to GM Jody Forman

In 1998, Jody Forman left HILCO after three years of service, and an interim manager stepped in for a couple of months.

Jody Forman receiving a gift

A New GM

Manager Gerald Lemons (1999 - 2007)

In June of 1999, HILCO's Board of Directors hired Gerald Lemons as the new General Manager. Known as "Jerry" to the staff, he brought a highly structured approach to running the Co-op. He endorsed technology and looked to the future needs of the members. Larry Farquhar remembers, "Jerry brought a lot of technology and advances to the Co-op."

Bob Wilson says, "Jerry had a lot of leadership capabilities. Military. That's what he was."

"Jerry brought a lot of his military background with him," says Lea Sanders. "Follow orders, organized personnel files/records, memos on everything as opposed to talking about them or sticky notes. He was very interested in being a leader in the cooperative world. He definitely did not take the 'this is how we've always done it' approach."

Debbie recalls the whirlwind of change of the late '90s. "One of the things that has changed most, up until 1998 is we were all housed in the same building—the linemen, the office personnel, the management, the mechanics. We all saw one another everyday. We were a very, very close group. If something was going on in your life, everybody knew about it. We knew each other's spouses' names, all our kids' names. We knew most of the kids' birthdays, because we were all there when they were born. We were truly a family. Over the years that's what I miss the most, that we're not all together anymore."

As HILCO expanded, the linemen moved to their own building across town. And in 1999, the warehouse next door to the Brown-Reese building was remodeled into a new wing for the offices. Debbie says, "It was inevitable. We had all outgrown being in one place."

The Y2K Scare

The Y2K problem, also known as "The Millennium Bug," was a concern that digital documentation and data storage would be lost when computer clocks rolled over from 1999 to the year 2000. This caused a lot of stress as companies around the globe prepared for possible computer failures in their systems.

As Y2K drew closer, there was a lot of apprehension at HILCO of what was going to happen when the flip happened. No one knew for sure if there was going to be a big power outage or not, but they prepared themselves. On New Year's Eve of 1999, HILCO employees camped out at the office and several substations ready to troubleshoot in case the Y2K flip caused any system-wide outages. As the clock approached midnight, everyone held their breath. Then, as the computers rolled over into the new millennium, nothing bad happened. The power continued to run along the power lines like clockwork, and everyone breathed a sigh of relief. The same occurred for businesses across the globe, as the Y2K scare turned out to be nothing more than a widespread fear of the unknown.

The 1990s was a decade of economic expansion both on Wall Street and in American households. Poverty decreased and personal incomes doubled from an earlier recession.

President Bill Clinton served two terms, surviving impeachment from the Whitewater controversy and an extramarital scandal with his intern, Monica Lewinsky. TV shows like *Baywatch*, *Friends*, *Seinfeld*, and *The Simpsons* were long-standing favorites. And video games played on home systems became popular among the younger generations.

While other co-ops around the nation were leveling off, HILCO continued to grow its membership. By the year 2000, there were 16,016 active members, an increase of over 4,000 members in ten years.

"A great many people experience the movement from one century to the next, but a minuscule number of people experience the movement from one millennium to the next."

— Neile Donald Walsch

"This young century will be liberty's century."

— President George W. Bush
July 15, 2005

CHAPTER TEN

The 2000s:
A New Millennium

While the 1990s had been the decade of the internet and a boost in the economy, the 2000s, during President George W. Bush's two terms, was a decade that the U.S. got a reality check and discovered even as a world super power the country has vulnerabilities. It started with 9/11, when planes flown by Muslim terrorists crashed into New York's Twin Towers and the Pentagon in Arlington, Virginia. Terrorism had a new face with Osama Bin Laden, and the U.S. focused on Homeland Security and a new War on Terror. In 2003, U.S. armed forces invaded Iraq and quickly ended Saddam Hussein's tyranny. This led to American troops occupying Iraq to help reform their government and bring democracy to the Middle East. Meanwhile, U.S. soldiers and marines fought another war over in Afghanistan. Known as Operation Enduring Freedom, U.S. and British armed forces invaded Afghanistan to dismantle a terrorist group known as Al-Qaeda, as well as the Taliban regime.

The 2000s was also a decade of global financial crisis. On the home front, Corporate America's spending came under scrutiny with scandals like Enron and AIG. A recession hit the latter half of the decade, causing an increase in unemployment. American families had to tighten their belts and change careers, and many retired men and women went back to work to make ends meet.

On the World Wide Web, Google became the most used search engine, and social media changed how people socialized with one another. Millions of people around the globe posted personal profiles to websites like MySpace, Facebook, and Twitter, and uploaded videos to YouTube. Technology continued to soar thanks to Apple's launch of products like the iPod and iPhone, which has turned the cell phone into a handheld computer. Apple's iTunes revolutionized how people buy music, making the CD almost obsolete. In music, Rock 'n Roll seemed to fade away as Rap and Hip-Hop topped most of the charts.

With so much reality bombarding Americans through CNN and the Internet, people escaped to fantasy books like the *Harry Potter* series and movies like *Lord of the Rings*, *The Pirates of the Caribbean*, and a slue of movies based on comic book heroes.

In Itasca, Texas, HILCO Electric Cooperative, under the leadership of Jerry Lemons, rolled with the times and kept their focus on keeping up with industry changes, technological advancements, safety training, and continuing to bring great service to their growing membership. At the start of 2000 there were over 16,000 active members.

The New Girl in HR

Lea Sanders

In 2000, Lea Sanders came on board to work in the Human Resources department, handling the benefits and insurance. One of Lea's biggest challenges was identifying employees with their records. "Everybody, especially the linemen, had a nickname. It took me a couple of days to figure out when they were talking about a person who they were talking about. Ronnie Upchurch was "Rock." David Brackin was "Buck." Thomas Cheek, they called him "Chico." Gary Lewis was "Shorty." And Travis Sanders, they called "Lightfoot."

Left to Right from Top: Brady Anderson, Todd Anderson,
Jimmy Vasquez, Jason Patton, Lance Henkelman, John Houston,
Danny Lewis & Eric Kern

Cross-Training

HILCO offers a unique opportunity to its employees to cross-train and learn about other positions within the company. Lea says, "The Co-op does a lot of cross-training for employees who want to go out – mainly the inside people who desire to go out and see what a lineman does or what a collector does or a staker. It helps them understand where they fit in and why the questions are so important when they talk to our members. It's pretty interesting to see what somebody else does."

Gena Brooks

Gena Brooks, who works in the main office, says, "When I was in dispatch, I went out to see what it was like to work the lines, so I went with T.C. (Tommy Cox). In order for me to get into the truck, T.C. had to pack a milk carton. So every time I would get up in the truck, he'd go around and get the milk carton, put it on the ground for me to get in and out ... I don't know why it was so hard to get up in that bucket truck. My legs were too short."

HILCO bucket truck

Lea Sanders has also gone out with the linemen. "I've been in a bucket truck. I lifted it all the way up. It was pretty scary. At least forty or fifty feet."

Linemen raising the bucket to the pole

David "Buck" Brackin   Kenneth Upchurch makes
and crew at work   the meter base hot

Daniel Beam works on a Pad Mount

Milton Cranfill oversees the Right-of-Way crew

Brush cleared around poles

The Standoff

On June 23, 2000, a domestic dispute between a man and his girlfriend led to a standoff with police in the Bethel community west of Peoria. Early that morning, Edgar Lee Fitzgerald attacked his girlfriend with a hatchet, severing two fingers and cutting a third. The woman escaped, driving across the pasture to a neighbor's house. The neighbor rushed her to the hospital and notified the police.

Meanwhile, Edgar Fitzgerald shot his girlfriend's horse then prepared for battle. He lined his pick up truck, a trailer loaded with his tractor and shredder, and a second trailer behind his house as a shield. He leaned six rifles against a wall near a window. He called relatives telling them he wasn't going back to jail. Then he called his former brother-in-law and said, "Take care of my son if anything happens to me."

At 8:30 a.m., Deputy Coy West drove up to the man's farm house to search for the woman's little finger. He was greeted by two shots that blew out his window. The deputy called for backup and authorities from Hill County Sheriff's Department, the Waco police department, and a SWAT team arrived on the scene and surrounded the perimeter. Hill County Sheriff Brent Button was in charge. He formed a command post in a house across the pasture. His team called Edgar and made several attempts to convince him to surrender. But Edgar remained holed up. He lied and told the police he had his seven-year-old son with him, so Sheriff Button and his deputies remained cautious.

At 4:00 that afternoon, they decided to cut off Edgar's water and electricity.

Lineman Tommy Cox will never forget that day. "We got a call that I needed to turn off a transformer at this location and there was police and something going on there. So I turned off there on 3050 and was going down the road, and when I drove up, there was cop cars everywhere."

The deputies took Tommy into a house where several SWAT members were gathered. "It was a hot day. They wanted me to come out there and cut off the power, so to make the house hot and force him out of there."

Tommy climbed into an armored vehicle that the SWAT team had brought. "We rode down the side road, and I pointed out what we needed to do." The police asked Tommy if he could cut the power. "I said, 'Yeah, there ain't nothing to it.' It had a cutout over the top of the transformer and all I would have to do is take a long stick and hook into the cutout and pull it down and turn the power off to the trailer. I thought I could stand at the armored car and all he could do is shoot that stick or shoot at my feet." They drove back to the command post with a plan that Tommy would perform the task.

Jerry Lemons arrived on the scene. He saw Tommy was about to ride off in the armored vehicle and said he couldn't allow Tommy to put himself at risk of getting shot. "So I had to coach them," says Tommy. He told the officers how to remove the cutout and work the stick.

The SWAT team piled into the armored vehicle and drove down the long driveway to the farm house. Using Tommy's stick, they killed the transformer.

Tommy Cox standing with a SWAT sniper and police

On a country road a few hundred yards away, the authorities waited behind a row of police vehicles. "We could see the house pretty good," remembers Tommy. "We was close enough he could have picked us off. For a deer rifle, that's no distance at all for somebody that's a marksman."

A sniper dressed in camouflage and grass was ready to take out the gunman if needed. Tommy stood on the road and watched anxiously. "We was looking at the house and seeing if he was moving, and all of the sudden we heard a shot."

Edgar Fitzgerald opened fire on the lawmen, shooting six or seven shots with his rifle. Several rounds went through the walls of the house where the negotiators were posted and bullets pinged the sheriff's vehicle near Tommy. "We were all diving down under cars by the wheels, and there was this SWAT woman, and she rolled down. I got down behind the wheel of a car. And I told that SWAT woman, 'Ma'am, you better get over here by me behind this tire, or he can still shoot under the car.'

179

And so she rolled over and got by me. My adrenaline was flowing. He finally quit shooting. Nobody was hit." Moments later the man in the house started a fire inside his home. "And then all of the sudden we heard a shot rang out and then the house started blazing. And the house burnt up and he didn't come out."

Firemen found Edgar Lee Fitzgerald's charred body in the ash. A coroner later reported that a gun wound to his chest indicated that he had committed suicide after starting the fire. "It was a pretty exciting thing when all that happened." It was reported that the police never fired a shot. But as Tommy reflects, he can only shake his head and wonder if, during all that commotion, that SWAT sniper might have fired one lethal round.

Goodbye to a Loyal Board Member

Harry Frank Holland

In 2001, the longest standing board member, Harry Frank Holland, retired after forty years. He had worked on the board from June 14, 1960 through December 21, 2001.

Leadership Training

Back Row: Allen Howe, David Brackin, Gerald Lemons,
and Randy Cox. Front Row: Debra Cole, Lea Sanders,
and Paula Farquhar

While Gerald Lemons was GM, HILCO began training employees to become leaders. "Jerry was a big proponent of advancing your education," remembers Lea Sanders, "especially if you were going to become some sort of manager. And back in 2001-2002, we actually worked with Hill College and got approval for either Jerry or myself to be able to be considered faculty at Hill College." Both Lea and Jerry were certified to teach courses. Lea says, "We taught college classes here at the Co-op after hours. He encouraged people who wanted to move into supervisor positions to at least go and obtain the seven courses that would get you your Supervisory Certification. I believe it is a twenty-college-hour program. And so a number of people took these classes from us."

First group to receive NRECA Supervisory Certification

Adventures in Filmmaking

Several years ago HILCO was chosen to be one of the co-ops that was featured in a CoBank promotional video that they would send out to co-ops that were looking to use the bank for financing. Lea Sanders remembers, "They wanted to come onsite to (shoot the video) and they gave us a list of things. They showed up here. It was two guys from California who had come in that were going to be doing this filming and scouting for the film. They came up late Friday afternoon, so on Saturday I had to go out with them."

Video crew shooting at HILCO office

Lea was handed the responsibility of helping the producer and cameraman find locations to shoot. "We wanted to get a picture of power lines going up a hill or something rural like a cow in the picture. And I had to call the customer to make sure it would be okay for us to come out there. And I had to help find co-op members that might be utilized in this video. One of the things that they were looking for was a girl that was about fourteen years old but had really long hair so they could shoot a spot where she ran by and a fan was going to blow and you could see her hair. So I was looking for very specific people that were also members."

That Saturday Lea led the two filmmakers on a casting hunt for the right people. They tried going to businesses but didn't have much luck, so she tried a different route. "It happened that week was Antique Alley. It's basically a big garage sale that stretches between Grandview and Cleburne."

Antique Alley

"So I'm riding around with these guys and we're stopping at all these little flea markets that are set up along the way ... and talking to fourteen-year-olds, asking if their parents were around, if they'd like to be in this commercial. And the two (filmmakers) were buying stuff while they were there, saying, 'Oh, I'm gonna buy these real cowboy boots.' And our car is filling up with whatever they're buying along the way."

While they collected a lot of souvenirs at Antique Alley, they still hadn't found the right fourteen-year-old girl. They next drove across the county toward Maypearl. Lea laughs, "We ended up going to a renaissance fair, which is Scarborough Fair. And they thought maybe they'll have some people there. I did end up finding somebody and she was there with a school group, so I'm having to talk to her teacher. She was a daughter of a member." Once the video was cast, Lea had to get the members' permission to use the power lines on their properties and cut off the power for the shoot. "I had to talk to the customer and say, 'We're going to be at your place, is that okay?' And then I had to stage different things, like linemen being on the pole changing equipment." The video came off without a hitch, and Lea got an education in filmmaking. The filmmakers went back to California with suitcases packed with souvenirs from Texas.

Deregulation Coming

Deregulation is where a consumer can choose who they purchase their Energy from (Reliant, TXU, Ambit, etc.) but that energy runs over the distribution lines of whoever owns the infrastructure. Oncor owns distribution lines that actually attach to the consumer's home, but any energy company can serve those homes over Oncor's wires.

"A cooperative is not part of deregulation," says Debbie Cole, "so no other energy company can serve our Members over our distribution lines. During the late '90s, we all knew deregulation was coming. It was just a matter of when, and would the cooperatives be included? Many hours and trips were put into planning, contacting elected officials, and trying to determine how it would affect the structure of the cooperative. When all was said and done in January 2002, the cooperatives had the choice of whether to opt into competition or not. HILCO is only a distribution cooperative (wires only), but if cooperatives had been forced into deregulation, it would have totally changed the way we did business."

Tales from the Dispatching Office

Crystal Upchurch with her father, Ronnie

In 2004, Crystal Upchurch came on board to work as a dispatcher during the after hours at night and on weekends. "Mostly what I did was take payments or payment arrangements. People would call in and needed to pay their bill or couldn't pay their bill and wanted me to give them an extension order. New customers would call in and we would ask them to fill out the application to establish service."

One of the main roles of the dispatcher is to take calls for outages and notify the linemen who are on call. "When we had outages," says Crystal, "we'd call and coordinate all of that through the dispatching office. We usually had one of the guys' supervisors on call. And if we had an outage, we'd contact them. Depending on how big it was, they'd come in. Then they could (coordinate) the guys and we could just deal with the customers."

Crew working at a substation

Most outages were caused by storms, but occasionally animals got into the substations. David Brackin says, "A snake could crawl back there, crawl on in, get into the line and knock the substation out. We've had birds do it, frogs and snakes, raccoons, buzzards. When they land in a substation, because it's so close together, they'll get into something. Now the outer part of the substation has an electric fence. If a snake crawls across that wire it kills them. They never have a chance to get to the substation."

Crystal says, "And, of course, we've had people digging and cut into lines. Mostly it's storms blowing transformers."

Nights on the Graveyard Shift

Often times Crystal worked alone or with one other employee in the building. "If we worked a day on the weekend, nobody was here." The dispatchers were stationed in the back part of the building. "We had surveillance cameras. One went on the front of the building. One went on the back of the building. And one in the front lobby pointed towards the door. I never looked at that one. Somebody could have just broken in. I never did look at that one. I'd be afraid of what I saw on that thing."

What spooked Crystal most was knowing that part of the building used to be a funeral parlor where Mr. Farrow had done embalming on dead people. "I was like, forget this. I'm not coming on that side of the building unless I absolutely have to. And I locked myself up in that room. And we had a little space heater. I would plug that thing in and that room would be so hot in the morning. Either Vivian or Mark would be the first ones to come in and they would just say, 'Ah, Crystal! It's so hot in here!' It was probably 80-85 by the time they came in. And I was like, 'No, it's cold in here.'"

"Be Advised: Vicious Dog in Backyard"

Some nights Crystal talked on the radio with employees who were working the late shift out in the field. "There was a guy that called me one night. He was disconnecting meters. He called me on the big radio and said that he was at this house, and the meter was in the backyard. And there is a vicious dog that is guarding the meter and he cannot get in there. He needed the lineman on-call, which was already home, to come out and disconnect, because these people were stealing electricity. They had pulled the fuse, I guess, and he was just going to pull the whole meter out. So he needed a lineman to come out and take it down. So I called the lineman, John Houston. And he said, 'Is he serious?'

"At the time Jerry Lemons was the manager here and he had heard us talking, the meter guy talking with the office. And (Jerry) called me and said, 'Hey, we're not going to have any problems here. You need to contact the police and have them meet there. And tell the gentleman that he needs to stay there and help the lineman, because I'm not sending out a second lineman. The police will meet him and we're going to take care of it.'

"So I do all that," Crystal continues, "and the lineman is calling me. And the meter guy, every time he'd come over the radio and say, 'Truck twenty-one to base. Be advised I'm sitting in the bank parking lot. Be advised there's a vicious dog. Or be advised I have the police officer.' And the lineman was on the telephone saying, 'Will you tell him to stop saying "be advised?"' And I would say to the meter man, 'Look, just deal with it all right. Just get out there and do the thing.' And Jerry's monitoring this and he's telling me, 'I want you to contact all through the radio so I can hear what's going on.' I had to call Rita, the supervisor, I had to tell her what was going on."

Crystal laughs. "The sheriff meets them, and they all go out to this house. And in a little bit, Jerry comes over the radio and says, 'Do we have a status update? What's going on?' The lineman gets on the radio and says, 'Be advised. The vicious dog in the back yard is a cocker spaniel.'"

189

Lending a Helping Hand

HILCO linemen helping firemen

Whenever fires, hurricanes, or tornados cause catastrophic damage, the electric co-ops pitch in and help out the community and one another. HILCO has contributed line crews to a good number of its neighboring co-ops. "It's just a family deal for co-ops," says lineman Travis Sanders, who has performed relief work in towns around Houston and the Gulf Coast that were heavily damaged by Hurricanes Katrina, Rita, and Ike. "If we're not hurting any in our co-op for sending us off, they go down there and try to help everybody else get their lines on."

Travis Sanders repairing a line

Once the line crews reach the town, they help in any way needed. In August 2005, they responded to the call after Hurricane Katrina devastated most of the Gulf Coast in Louisiana. They mostly climbed poles where bucket trucks couldn't reach. Travis recalls, "They had contractors going down the main line, the three-phase line, and getting that back up and repaired. And the linemen would take each tap, which was a single-phase built off (the main line) where trees fell through it, and we'd go through there climbing.

It's a lot different style of work. You don't know where you're at. I know on (our) system I pretty much know every place on it. Then you put me in a place I've never seen before and I don't know where the lines feed from. Basically, you can get put on 100 or 200 acres of power line in New Orleans or whatnot."

The summer of 2005 turned out to be a tumultuous hurricane season as Hurricane Rita struck the Gulf Coast again just weeks after Katrina, this time destroying buildings, homes, and power lines in towns all around Houston. While working in Livingston, Travis couldn't believe all the things he saw. "They had tent cities where they put up big circus tents. Everybody is just laying up underneath those. I had never seen a gas station completely emptied. Several restaurants closed. The first day we was there it was almost empty, and then after that it was like a mad house. There were people arguing. The whole store looked like a bomb went off in it. Everything was emptied or stepped on: dirty diapers, gas cans, people lined up for a mile trying to get fuel. I'd never seen anything like that. That was the worst." For HILCO's line crew it was like they had traveled to a third world country. Travis says, "We were staying in a motel with no lights, no water for thirty-two days. Taking a bath in the swimming pool in a hundred-degree weather."

Their services would be needed again two years later. "Hurricane Ike was the last one I worked," says Travis, remembering the pandemonium. "There were contractors everywhere. We were working on a feeder south of town and these (guides), we call them "bird dogs"—they lead us around from job to job telling us what to do. Well, he started talking to these two guys in a bucket, and the guys in the bucket didn't understand what the guy was telling him, that we were going to be working on the line. And they said we needed to go talk to their foreman." As it turned out the contracted crew had been working on the wrong power lines for two days. Travis and the other HILCO linemen who went with him dealt with a lot of chaos but did their part to restore power to the small towns.

HILCO's First Female GM

Debra Cole (Manager 2007 - Present)

In 2007, Gerald Lemons left HILCO and this time the Board of Directors was more forward thinking when they chose to hire their next GM from within the company. Debbie Cole had the right combination of work ethic, leadership skills, and experience in the electric power business. After rising up the branches from cashier to Assistant General Manager, she also had a well-rounded understanding of HILCO's culture and how the Co-op operated. The board members knew Debbie personally and could foresee that she would work in alignment with the board's goals for its members and the growth of the Cooperative.

She recalls, "When I became the General Manager/CEO I was a bit nervous, not because I didn't know the business, but because I had worked with most of these people for many years as a co-worker and there were only three other female Managers in the State of Texas. As usual, the employees of HILCO were there to help and support a fellow employee." Debbie transitioned into her new position just fine. "If it had not been for the staff, that first year would have been very rough, but now that I look back, it wasn't all that bad."

HILCO's office staff in 2008

Gene Farrow, son of the late Mr. Farrow, remembers a day he came to visit Debbie in her new office. "In the Brown-Reese building there's a wide staircase and her office is on the right. I went up there and started laughing, and she said, 'What's the matter?' And I said, 'Your office is where my dad used to do his embalming. And right across the hall was the conference room—that's where all the caskets were. People would go up and look for a casket.'" That was several decades ago, of course. The original furniture store and funeral parlor had been renovated over the years and now function as offices.

**Debbie posing in a bucket with grandson, Brayden Cole
and granddaughter, Gracee Cole**

Debbie stepped into the role of General Manager/CEO at a very exciting time for the power utility industry. She says, "It seems like I began this role when the playing field was in a major upgrade. Technology was flowing over from the office functions into the field functions."

Technological Advancements

Since 2000, HILCO has kept up with industry changes and advanced their technology in ways that have increased efficiency and saved money for the Co-op. One of the most important improvements is switching over to the SCADA System. SCADA, an acronym for Supervisory Control and Data Acquisition, allows HILCO to monitor and control its power lines and meters from a centralized computer.

"SCADA is real convenient," says Debbie. "It keeps the linemen from having to drive the whole entire system to locate an outage."

David Brackin says, "We can look at the substations and operate the substations from the office. And now we're looking in the SCADA on all of our re-closers, regulators, and stuff like that. We can have an outage now in Glenn Heights substation and I can get on my computer and see what's out. I can operate the re-closer and everything from the office. That's just one of the main things that's come about that's going to really be nice."

Assistant Director of Operations David Brackin

William Watson says, "With the SCADA, it deals with the main power lines, and you can cut off an entire area. I can sit at my computer and turn power lines off, turn them on, and change settings. I can set what we call a 'one shot,' where somebody's working on the line. We put the utilities on one shock absorber. If they have any contact, the line shuts off. We can see what the load is on the line anytime. See what the power factor on the line is. This is all right now just at the substation breakers. We're in the process of moving down-line with this control to our regulators, so we can keep the power quality at its peak."

There is also the TWACS system, which is the two-way communication with individual meters. Lea Sanders says, "In the past, people would call in outages and linemen would have to go to those locations and try to figure out where the problem might be. And now with the outage management we're able to start automatically contacting those meters and the meters directly upstream to see if they have power. And if they don't have power they can go upstream from that until they get to a device so they can find where the problem starts. And we can talk to any of those meters hooked into a substation and the meters can talk back to us."

William Watson posing with TWACS system at a substation

David Brackin smiles at how much technology has changed from when he was a lineman. "When I was out in the field, we'd take a week off and read meters. Then they got the meter readers. That's all they did was read meters from different cycles."

The installation of SCADA, TWACS/AMR meters (Automated Meter Reading) simplified an entire department. "You don't have meter readers anymore," says David. "It eliminated the position. They moved all of them into different positions in different departments. Now we read meters from the computers. Our meter reading system. We just have one man now. If a meter is not reading and there's something wrong with it, he'll go out and check it. Just one man. That cut down on a lot of time and driving."

Thomas Cheek working with SCADA

Lea Sanders says, "People remember when they used to have a meter reader come to their house once a month and visit with them while they were there, and now it's gone to just being automated. We've also gained a lot of efficiency, because we can get daily readings which can help members understand their usage patterns. We can line that up with temperatures."

Debbie Cole says, "When I came in to be a general manager, it was at a time that the industry was changing a lot. Technology had been pushed inside the office for years and years, but now technology is booming out in the field. You have your advanced mapping systems. You have your PCs in the linemen's trucks."

"Everybody has their own computer," says Travis Sanders. "We use those for email (and) to get our service orders. As long as you're by one of our substations you can hook up and get back to the office. And we got our maps on there and our fusing charts. Like if we're working out on a line and we have a line out and the fuse is blown, we used to have to call into the office and get somebody to go to the map and see what size fuse to put back in it. But now you can just look on your computer at the maps. But mainly we use them for communicating back with our main office and the operations office."

HILCO crew member working on a field computer

The latest and most exciting technology is GPS. Where linemen used to have to pull out a large map book to locate poles or a member's house, they now can find them on a computerized map grid. Lea remembers when the GPS system was being installed. "We hired a crew, and it took them about 2.5-3 years, and they started at the substations and every pole has a coordinate for it and it can map in all the way to the end point, to the meters."

New Equipment

HILCO continually updates its equipment as needed. Travis Sanders says, "Probably in the last ten years or so we've advanced in our equipment. When I first got hired and got put on a crew, we only had one bucket and one digger. We probably didn't have more than four or five buckets overall. Now we have eleven or twelve bucket trucks."

Linemen working with bucket trucks

The size of HILCO's workforce has grown over the years. Back in the '60s they only had around twelve linemen. Today, there are about twenty-five linemen on the force.

David Brackin says, "We've got a contracting brush crew and then two crews on the pipe for construction. And we've got one underground crew. Of course, we've got our own HIL-CO construction crew. And an underground crew. They don't do any digging. They just do the final connect. And then, of course, the service guys. You have to go to school and learn about all the equipment changes. You always have to be updating yourself. Stay up with what's changing."

"We have two diggers," says Travis Sanders, "a pressure digger and a boom-style digger. The pressure digger is more for rocks. It's got the weight and the bit right off the rear end of the truck where you can pick up the weight of the truck to dig. And the other one's a boom-chip style digger. It's got an arm where you can reach out anywhere from twelve foot to twenty foot. We also have an alley machine. It looks like a mini digger on rubber tracks. You can put a bucket on it and work out of the bucket or you can use it to dig holes for the set poles. We use it in tight situations."

Lance Henkelman with a digger bit

Ronnie and Kenneth Upchurch working a digger

Safety Training

HILCO Pole Climbing School

Linemen are constantly learning about safety. David Brackin, who has led numerous safety meetings, says, "We have our safety meetings once a month. It lasts half a day. Of course, we always have bucket training and bucket rescue. Pole-top rescue. We do that every year.

"Safety is number one here with us," continues David. "They are coming out with a new safety strap that's supposed to keep you from falling. You put it around the pole and it goes on the inside of the pole too. When you fall, you're weight locks it to the pole."

Milton Cranfill practicing pole rescue

Another change over the past decade is the clothing they wear. "When you work," says David, "you have to have your safety glasses, a shield, your hard hat, and your flame retarded clothes on. It's just pants and a shirt that are treated with some chemical that won't burn. That way if you get a flash on your body, it won't catch your clothes on fire. And steel-toe boots. And 20,000 or 30,000 KV rubber gloves."

Wade Howard wearing safety gear

Even the size of the wires have changed. "It's funny," says Kenneth Upchurch. "When we first started going with Dad to work (back in the Fifties), if they go out to build a line, they'd carry 3-kVA." KVA stands for Kilo Volt Ampere or Amps. "If they carried a five out, that was big. And then if you carried a 25-kVA out, that was unheard of as far as the load. Now, I doubt they have anything smaller than a twenty-five. Maybe for very few occasions. The system, everything has changed so much. The equipment that they work with now is so much safer."

Better Infrastructure

Substation

Since the Co-op first started building power lines in 1937, HILCO has done their part to swap out a lot of the original poles and lines. David says, "Now we've got more substations. Bigger wire. Our poles are closer together. They were anywhere from 300 to 350 feet. Now, we don't get them over 300. Most of the time we try to go from 250 to 300. Bigger poles than we used to use. Back then you had a Class-six pole. Now we use Class-four and fives. Bigger poles and more weight, just stronger. You just beef your system up, but you have to do that because of the wire size. The wire, you've got to hold it. We've got more three-phase than we ever had. A lot of people still want that."

The Lineman's Rodeo

Wade Yarbro, Gary Lewis, Travis Sanders and Allen Howe

Every year a group of HILCO linemen compete in the Texas Lineman's Rodeo in Seguin, Texas, as well as others like the International Lineman's Rodeo in Kansas City, Kansas.

"It's more of a safety and training event," says William Watson. "It's not just Co-ops. Municipals and I.O.Us participate in it too."

Bob Wilson says, "People bring their lawn chairs and sit out and watch it."

William says, "My son, (Kristopher Watson), worked as a lineman here for many years. He was the first participant for HILCO in the Lineman's Rodeo. That would have been the early '90s."

HILCO linemen competing at the 2010 rodeo in Seguin, Texas

The linemen who compete do it on a voluntary basis. "We don't tell them that they have to go," says David Brackin. "We sponsor them. Normally it's around eight. The ones that do it, actually do the climbing and everything. And then we have some alternates, like a couple in case somebody gets hurt or gets sick. They'll take their place. We have a couple of judges that go every year. It's a pretty good turn out."

Travis Sanders, who has competed in the event as well as been a judge, says, "Last year I did one in Stephenville and then in Seguin. We did lots of practicing. Started in February and practiced once or twice a week from February to July."

Wade Yarbro and Travis Sanders
competing at a rodeo

In 2010, First Class Linemen Jason Patton, Lance Henkelman, and Kane Montgomery represented HILCO Electric in the Texas Linemen's Rodeo in Seguin. Apprentice Linemen Chris Brown and Clayton Thompson competed in the Apprentice Division. John Houston, John Prescott, and Travis Sanders helped with the judging. Other HILCO employees who came out to volunteer and support the teams were General Manager/CEO Debra Cole, Assistant General Manager Lea Sanders, Underground Foreman and Rodeo Coordinator B.J. Williams, Thomas Cheek, and Milton Cranfill.

Left to right: Milton Cranfill, John Prescott, Thomas Cheek, Chris Brown, Clayton Thompson, Lance Henkelman, Kane Montgomery, John Houston, Jason Patton and Travis Sanders

Lance Henkelman and Kane Montgomery racing the clock

Jason Patton assists his teammates from the ground

At the Seguin rodeo, Patton, Henkelman, and Montgomery made history in 2010. They outperformed twenty-seven other teams, winning first place Journeyman Team in the Cooperative Division. They placed second in the Overall Journeyman competition.

Winning Journeyman Team: Jason Patton, Lance Henkelman, and Kane Montgomery

HILCO's Commitment to the Community

Tasha Bell and Bob Wilson helping the charity Angels on the Move

Cathy Farquhar volunteering for The Salvation Army

HILCO sponsoring "Relay for Life" for American Cancer Society

Raising the Flag

213

HILCO Helping Students

HILCO offers a scholarship program that awards college scholarships to students. Debbie Cole says, "The kids fill out applications and they are awarded based on need and overall application qualifications."

Director Ron Roberts and President of the Board Bill Allen present a college scholarship to Demsey Bonner

HILCO also offers a Youth Tour to Washington, D.C. for students. Debbie says, "For several years HILCO has sponsored two high school students on a June trip to Washington D.C. with other students from all across the U.S. Cooperative employees serve as chaperons (staff from HILCO has taken their turn with this duty) for the group of students. Usually in March the students from schools in our CCN are asked to submit a 500-word essay, relating to some topic of 'What it means to be an American.' The essays are then judged blind by a selected panel of judges and two students are awarded an all-expense, week-long trip to Washington D.C. where they learn the functions of our government and meet and bond with other students from all over the U.S."

**Youth Tour Winners: Heather Myers
and Andrea Palmer in D.C.**

HILCO's Commitment to Its Members

Each year HILCO continues to host two annual picnics for its members, one in Waxahachie for its northern districts and one down in West for the southern districts. Barbecue is typically catered. Entertainment includes live music and door prizes. The picnics are also an opportunity for the members to meet HILCO employees and board members face to face.

Today's Board of Directors is more heavily involved with nearly every facet of the Cooperative. Not only do they attend regular meetings to discuss current projects and the future direction of the Co-op, the board members also pay close attention to the changes in the electric power industry and advancements in technology. They make trips to Washington to discuss political and legal issues that affect electric co-ops. And they take courses, seminars, and earn certifications to further their education about the always-changing electric power industry.

Like the original pioneers who started up the co-ops, today's Board has a continuing passion and commitment of in-

suring that Rural America stays on track to be as technological-
ly advanced as cities and suburbs. Thanks to the Board, HILCO
continues to expand and grow every year.

HILCO's Board of Directors, from top left: Joseph Tedesco,
Vice President George Thiess, President Bill Allen, Ron Roberts,
Stephen Pape, Janet Smith, and Secretary/Treasurer Margaret Hill

The 2000s has been another decade of positive growth. By
2009, HILCO had 22,683 active members, an increase of 6,667
meters in 9 years. The competition between Hill County and
Ellis County continued. By June 2010, Hill County was leading
by 558 members.

CHAPTER ELEVEN

2012 and Beyond:
Continuing Mr. Farrow's Dream

The year 2012 is a monumental period in many scientific circles. It marks the end of the Mayan calendar. Astronomers believe it is a time of great planetary change. Some philosophers see this year as a time of transition, while others view it as a dawn of new possibilities. For the employees, Board of Directors, and members of HILCO, 2012 is a year to celebrate the anniversary of 75 years of being a part of a great electric cooperative.

HILCO began back in 1937 with one man's dream to bring power to the rural people. During a time when America was still dealing with the Great Depression, when utility companies were selective on who they would deliver power to, Earl Farrow decided to make a difference. Taking a leap of faith, he borrowed money from the REA and started up Hill County Electric Cooperative. With the support of his board members and just two employees, Mr. Farrow built the Co-op from the ground up. He created jobs for the local people living in and around Itasca. He oversaw the building of power lines across Central Texas to farms the other utility companies wouldn't reach. His co-op electrified the first rural houses in five counties.

Mr. Farrow brought to the Cooperative a solid foundation, family values, and a determination to bring great electric service to the members who made up the Co-op. His traditions of family have carried on over the years. Today, the staff has grown to over eighty employees, membership has surpassed 22,000 members, and the technologies have advanced into the Twenty First Century. And while the name has changed to HILCO, the heart and soul of the Cooperative has remained the same as the day it began 75 years earlier. The Board of Directors continues to represent the members and steers the course of the Co-op in a direction that best serves its members.

Mr. Farrow's son, Gene, says, "On this 75th Anniversary of the Cooperative, I am sure that Earl is looking down, telling all who have served and those who are serving the communities between Waco and Dallas, 'Well done and keep the dream alive.'"

Mr. Farrow left behind more than a legacy of delivering power to people. He taught us that when you set forth with a dream to make a difference in the lives of others, dreams can come true.

APPENDIX

The People of HILCO

Staff at main headquarters in Itasca

Itasca headquarters staff: Bob Wilson, Joe Marek,
Hollis Cunningham, Kathleen Carter

HILCO's Board of Directors, from top: Stephen Pape, Janet Smith,
George Thiess, Bill Allen, Margaret Hill,
Joseph Tedesco, and Ron Roberts

Operations and Engineering

Sam Forbus, Shane Edwards, and Rick Baskett

225

The Whitney Office Staff, back: Peggy Young, Danny Smith,
Sam Wilson, Tommy Bradley, Victor Canales
and Jeremiah Auvenshine. Front: Saralynn Ainsworth,
Lacey Warren, Will Garnett, and Shane Rogers

The Midlothian Office Staff: Lauren Dillon,
Loren Odle, and Michelle Rickett

HILCO Legends Retire

Payroll Clerk Louise Wilson & Carolyn Bons

**2006 retirement party for Ronnie Upchurch (40 years)
& Kenneth Upchurch (28 years)**

In August 2008, brothers Danny Lewis (left) retired after 32 years
and Gary "Shorty" Lewis (right) retired after 35 years

In March 2011 William Watson retired after 48 years

Special thanks to Margaret Rhea
who has preserved much of the Co-op's history

And special thanks to Attorney Martha McGregor
who has been serving HILCO since 1993

229

About the Author

Brian Moreland writes non-fiction, novels, and short stories of supernatural suspense. In 2007, his novel *Shadows in the Mist*, a Nazi Occult thriller set during World War II, won a gold medal for Best Horror Novel in an international contest. It went on to publish in Germany under the title *Schattenkrieger*. His second novel, *Dead of Winter*, a historical horror set in Canada, released October 2011. When not working on books, Brian edits documentaries and TV commercials around the globe. He produced a World War II documentary in Normandy, France and worked at two military bases in Iraq with a film crew. He is the son of Patti and Keith Moreland, both HILCO Members. Brian lives in Dallas, Texas where he is diligently writing his next novel. You can communicate with him online at www.BrianMoreland.com or on Twitter @BrianMoreland.

CPSIA information can be obtained at www.ICGtesting.com
Printed in the USA
LVOW060947251011

251992LV00002B/4/P